WITH

MARGARET MORGAN
and
MARY MORGAN PEDLOW

Memorial

RIVERSIDE PUBLIC LIBRARY

AMERICAN LIBRARY ASSOCIATION
Chicago and London 1998

The author acknowledges permission to reprint an excerpt from "Reading Room, The New York Public Library," from COLLECTED POEMS 1930–1986 by Richard Eberhart. Copyright © 1960, 1976, 1987 by Richard Eberhart. Used by permission of Oxford University Press, Inc.

Cover by Baugher Design

Cover photo of rock garden, Ryoan-ji Temple, Kyoto, by the author

Design and composition by Dianne M. Rooney in Stemple Schneidler using QuarkXpress 3.32

Printed on 55-pound Windsor Book, a pH-neutral stock, and bound in 12-point coated cover stock by Patterson Printing

The paper used in this publication meets the minimum requirements of American National Standard for Information Sciences—Permanence of Paper for Printed Library Materials, ANSI Z39.48-1992.

Library of Congress Cataloging-in-Publication Data
Gorman, Michael, 1941–
    Our singular strengths : meditations for
librarians / by Michael Gorman ; decorations by
Emma Gorman.
      p.   cm.
   ISBN 0-8389-0724-5 (alk. paper)
   1. Library science—United States.   I. Title.
Z665.2.U6G67   1998
020—dc21   97-34547

Printed in the United States of America.

02 01 00 99 98   5 4 3 2 1

This book is dedicated to my mother
    Alicia Gorman
and my grandson
    Louis Dexter Gorman

Contents

Two
Values

Three
Lives

Four
Laws

Five
Change, Problems, and Realities

Eight
Places

Nine
Reading and Writing

Twelve
Eternal Promises

Preface

The Rinzai sect of Buddhism uses the *koan* as a means of reaching understanding. The *koan* is a paradox or puzzle that aids meditation and provides the insight that leads to enlightenment by freeing the mind from the constraints of reason. My Occidental life has made me a determined rationalist and I offer these meditations as upside-down koans—observations rooted in experience and reason that may provide insight into libraries, librarianship, and being a librarian today. The word *koan* means, literally, "public plan/proposal," and, taken together, these meditations offer such a plan or proposal for any librarian who may find it useful.

When I was presented with the idea of a book of meditations, I was ignorant of the genre. I looked at many such books and found myself interested in, and engaged by, one in twenty at most. I need not dwell on what did not attract me about most of the books. The form itself, however, I found intriguing. The style I chose for these meditations—a quotation, short essay, and resolution—is one that presents challenges and opportunities to the writer, not least the distillation of thought and economy of language. My aim is to present a topic, thought, or story that encapsulates some aspect of libraries and learning as an aid to understanding or reassessment. Beyond that I wish to provide aid and comfort to my colleagues in this profession that is often besieged—financially, psychologically, and in many other ways.

The resolutions at the end of each of the 144 meditations are offered, in all humility, both as a resolution of the issue discussed and a resolution that may assist the reader in thinking like a librarian, being a librarian, or just getting through the day. They seek to do nothing more than to suggest and assist in a helpful and positive way. I cannot claim any superior wisdom or more insight than anyone else and write colleague to colleague in the full knowledge that thinking about and writing each of these essays made me realize how much I have to learn and how far to travel.

My forty years of work in libraries have created a set of beliefs that underpin everything I do. I believe passionately in libraries—in their social and cultural value, their redemptive power, and their centrality to learning and civilization. I believe in the intelligent use of technology to enhance the services and programs of libraries and to enable us to fulfill our historic mission. I believe in real, not virtual, libraries. I believe in our core values of service, intellectual freedom, and the right of all to equal and full library services. I believe that reading is a vital component of human progress and that we do no more important things than giving the habit of reading to children and encouraging ever-increasing literacy in adults. I believe in public service and the public good and in the profession of librarianship, which has made so many contributions to both. I believe that all libraries and librarians share a common purpose and that solidarity and mutual assistance should be among our guiding professional lights. If this book, in expressing these beliefs, can make some contribution to librarianship and individual library lives, it will have been well worth the writing.

Michael Gorman
Fresno, April 1997

Acknowledgments

I would like to thank, first of all, my friend and editor sans pareil Art Plotnik. He encouraged me to write this book, commented extensively on each of the drafts, and improved both style and content. He is not responsible for any shortcomings that remain. I would also like to thank my assistant, Susan Mangini, and student assistant and accomplished flautist, Carrie Zimmerman, for their invaluable help in preparing the final manuscript. Ideas, comments, and advice came from many friends and colleagues; I am grateful for their interest and friendship and hope they will find echoes and resonance in these pages. I am particularly grateful to Provost Alexander Gonzalez, my boss and friend, who granted me the administrative leave that I needed to complete this book. As ever, I am blessed by the love of my daughters, Emma and Alice, and the way it illuminates even the darkest days.

One

Beginnings & Endings

Opening the Door

*There are possibilities in a door always, for
how can you know what is on the other side?*

—Anthony Hope, *Tales of Two People*

 I open the doors of the library at eight each weekday
morning. One automatic door and three others. I say
"Good morning" to at least the first of those who
enter and to the recognized regulars. I tell anyone who asks
why I open the doors that these are the only minutes of the
day in which a library director can feel truly useful. The truth
is that I am reliving the time when, as a sixteen-year old
"junior assistant," I used to open the doors of a small public
branch library in North London. It seemed to me then and it
seems to me now that opening the library to its community is
of great symbolic as well as obviously practical importance.
What is it that releases the energy and the power we have
gathered and made available? The presence of the people on
whose behalf we work.

*I will take pleasure in the simple tasks
of my work.*

Library Furniture

. . . set thee right,
  Turn'd thy darkness into light.

—William Cowper, *Olney Hymns*

 One of my earliest library memories is of the contrast between the heavy, massive, dark furniture of the "lending library" and the low, light furniture in the children's library of my local public library. The lending library was for adults and seemed to set out to impress its patrons in the integration of all that dark wood with the vaguely church-like architecture of its rooms. The children's library, on the other hand, was scaled down and even the adults who worked there sat behind low desks on blond wood chairs or on bright cloth-covered tuffets to read to us at story hour.

Over the years, the taste for liturgical darkness in library furniture has waned and been replaced by a Scandinavian aesthetic of light colors, clean lines, and an absence of ornament. Now, it is not only children who are allowed light and color. Modern libraries have become welcoming, almost playful places with furniture to match. One of my first tasks was to thread daily newspapers on to heavy dark sticks with carved ends so they could reside in large racks waiting to be read. If the idea was to echo the atmosphere of a Viennese coffeehouse, it failed. The newspaper sticks and racks were just another ponderous note in the Victorian gloom. I am glad that we have swapped the solidity of that old, well-made furniture for the less sturdy, lighter desks, tables, chairs, racks, and shelves of today.

> *I will make my library a place*
> *of color and light.*

4

Celebrating Diversity

And if every flower looked just the same,
"Flower" would have to be each flower's name.

—Eugene Fern, *Pepito's Story*

 Pepito, the hero of Eugene Fern's story, is a little boy who loves to dance and is seen as "different" by the people who live in his town. When the mayor's daughter falls ill, each child is asked to bring a gift to cheer her up. Pepito brings the only gift he has—his dancing—and the magic of his talent helps her to recover from her illness. The lesson of this lovely children's book is that diversity and difference are valuable to communities and should be cherished, never shunned. Diversity (of language, color, religion, ethnicity, culture, opinion, styles of living) is important to every aspect of libraries and library work. Our collections should be diverse; our staff diverse; our users diverse in this place where a thousand, thousand flowers bloom and all are welcome to enjoy all opinions and all of the cumulative experience of humankind.

I will celebrate diversity in all aspects
of library experience.

The Library Journal, 1915

*Our chief interest in the past is as a guide
to the future.*

—W. R. Inge, *Assessments and Anticipations*

 I cast my net widely in searching for quotations for these pieces. A friend recommended that I look at the little "fillers" that grace the pages of old issues of the *Library Journal.* Almost at random, I looked at the 1915 bound volume of *LJ* and found a number of items such as "A library has been said to be a true university; it is also a fairyland, a haven of repose from the storms and troubles of the world" (Lord Avebury) but I also had a glimpse into another world in these elegantly printed pages. Whole theses could be stimulated by the "Imperial Public Library, St Petersburg," "How far should the library aid the peace movement and other propaganda?" and "The status of the library in Southern high schools."

Contributors included some of the great names of American library history—Isadore Gilbert Mudge, J. C. M. Hanson, Julia Pettee, and R. R. Bowker. The monthly news sections showed the great march of Carnegie libraries across the country, the growth of university libraries, and the high-minded industry that was building libraries and collections everywhere. The Oakland, Kansas, library (slogan, "A book for every home, a book for every person") received 1,000 quarters in three days. Miss Elizabeth Tough discussed story hours with the Missouri Valley Library Club. Charles Martel used the pages to engage others in a furious debate on cataloguing rules. All this energy and idealism on pages that are as read-

able today as they were more than eighty years ago in volumes that bear the plate of the Hutchinson (Kansas) Public Library!

> *I will study the past to understand the present
> and to know the future.*

First Day at Work

 I am much nearer my last day of work than my first, but I remember the latter with crystal clarity: the weather, time of day, traveling to the library on the bus, the people I met, where I went for lunch, and that odd feeling of leaving at the end of the day knowing that I would be back the next morning. All that and surrounded by books! I learned early that actually spending time with individual books was not part of the job description, but it was a pleasure to have them there and to be an insider learning the mechanics of libraries, how those familiar places worked.

That was a different time and in another country, but surely that first day of work and the first days in new places thereafter are remembered by us all with a vividness that comes from a world that was full of possibilities. Even as jobs become careers and as we learn more about libraries, people, and life, we still remember that first day, that first step of a long journey. Even after many years we can recapture wonder, recall that sense of limitlessness, and, in remembering, rekindle enthusiasm and remind ourselves of what might yet be.

*I will remember and rekindle the excitement
of my first day at work.*

"The Money Is There for Technology"

Americans have been conditioned to accept newness, whatever it costs them.

—John Updike, *A Month of Sundays*

 Library users continue to use "traditional" collections and services to a much greater extent than they do electronic resources. Even the highest priests of information technology will admit that such technology and what they are pleased to call "traditional" collections (books and the like) and services are equally important for today and tomorrow. I asked a public librarian friend why it is that requests for extra funding for "technology" were more numerous than requests for extra funds for books and other tangible collections. She said "The money is there for technology," a fact that makes us all followers of the philosopher Willie Sutton. I can attest to the fact that technological projects are much more "sexy" to most university administrators than are other library programs. We have brought much of this upon ourselves. In an effort to go with the flowing tide, we have downplayed the importance of printed materials and other library collections and services. The right and effective political thing to do would be to boost both books and technology and argue that we need the yin of one and the yang of the other. We would transform ourselves into happy political warriors and cease to be prisoners of a defeatism acquiescing in distorted funding.

I will fight for equitable support for needed services, "traditional" or high tech.

First Books

I had a passion for reading, especially for Horatio Alger stories. I went to the public library almost every day and, when I found a Horatio Alger book I had not read before, it was like finding a gold mine.

—William S. Paley, *As It Happened: A Memoir*

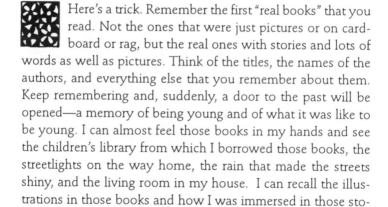 Here's a trick. Remember the first "real books" that you read. Not the ones that were just pictures or on cardboard or rag, but the real ones with stories and lots of words as well as pictures. Think of the titles, the names of the authors, and everything else that you remember about them. Keep remembering and, suddenly, a door to the past will be opened—a memory of being young and of what it was like to be young. I can almost feel those books in my hands and see the children's library from which I borrowed those books, the streetlights on the way home, the rain that made the streets shiny, and the living room in my house. I can recall the illustrations in those books and how I was immersed in those stories and characters—lost in the living of what I was reading that comes so easily to children and is so rare in adults.

I have talked to a number of people about their first books, and in every case—including mine—those books were a mixture of "classics" *(Alice in Wonderland, Little House on the Prairie, Anne of Green Gables)* and the kind of books, now mostly forgotten, that neither aspired to nor won awards. What matters is the experience of living other lives through reading. Our

10

memories of early reading are as sharp and sweet whether the book remembered is *The Hobbit* or a Nancy Drew mystery.

I will rekindle the excitement of reading by recalling my first books.

The Solace of Knowledge

At the age of 18, I found myself pregnant
and afraid. I wasn't alone but afraid of not
knowing what was happening to my body. The
Livonia branch kept me out of the dark. I read
everything on childbirth, including the natural.
Reading helped me to prepare myself for the
birth of my first daughter.

—Linda Santell (Redford, Michigan), quoted in the
ALA national campaign *Libraries Change Lives*

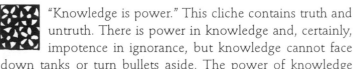 "Knowledge is power." This cliche contains truth and untruth. There is power in knowledge and, certainly, impotence in ignorance, but knowledge cannot face down tanks or turn bullets aside. The power of knowledge arises first from the ability to know the world better, know more about one's circumstances, and know what others have done when the circumstances in their lives were similar. Beyond the practical applications of knowledge lie the means to "know then thyself" and to build upon knowledge to create new circumstances, new lives. It is hard to overestimate the importance of libraries as repositories of knowledge for those faced with life's difficulties, particularly young people without the life experience that could enable them to overcome those difficulties.

Many biographies tell us of persons of achievement who, when young, felt themselves to be "different" (because they were shy, artistic, bookish, gay, religious, or just overcome by the splendors and miseries of life) and found in the local library a place of refuge and consolation. The books that

libraries supply can ameliorate loneliness, validate difference, and make life seem worthwhile. Moreover, those books are supplied without value judgments or hindrance. A major social value of libraries can be found in these stories of unhappy young people who accomplished much later in their lives, in part because of the solace of the knowledge that they found in libraries.

> *I will provide library materials that can encourage and console.*

Your Pornography, My Erotica

I shall not attempt further to define the kinds of [pornographic] material . . . but I know it when I see it.

—Supreme Court Justice Potter Stewart,
June 22, 1964

 Libraries of all kinds come under attack because of books and other materials with a sexual content. Most of us have dealt with irate library users demanding the instant withdrawal of a "filthy" book that they have, in the interests of public morality, read very thoroughly. The test of freedom of expression is the defense of expression of which one disapproves. Nowhere is this dictum more applicable than in dealing with sexual texts and images. It is easy to defend works that are considered to be "literature," and those who would ban, say, D. H. Lawrence, J. D. Salinger, and even Anaïs Nin are more the objects of ridicule than fear. When it comes to erotic writings and images with minimal literary or artistic value . . . wait a minute! Who decides? Is there a certificate of literary value or a seal of approval for some nude photographs and not others? Of course not. We are left only with the bedrock principles that lead us, in the words of the Library Bill of Rights, to resist all ". . . abridgement of free expression and free access to ideas"—no matter what our own views of that expression or those ideas may be.

I will avoid personal value judgments in defending free access.

14

Starved of Content

"Isn't that lovely?" she sighed. "It's my favorite program—fifteen minutes of silence."

—Norman Juster, *The Phantom Tollbooth*

 Reuven Frank, the former president of NBC News, is a still small voice in the clamor of the "information revolution." Examining the predictions of 200-, 300-, 500-channel television systems in the next few years, he asks why we should believe that these would result in anything but more home-shopping, more old movies, and more re-runs of old TV shows. Countering rhetoric with practicality, Mr. Frank asks from whence the new content for all these channels is to come. Even if the talent were available, who would produce, direct, act in, write, pay for, and distribute all the thousands of shows, documentaries, etc., that the 500 channels will demand? (Note that 500 channels will devour *12,000 hours* of programming each day.)

Frank's words made me think about the way other voices exalt the Internet as if its technological marvels are equaled by its accessible resources of general interest. The plain fact is that, on television and the Internet/Web, we are replete with technology and starved for thought-provoking, organized content. Political office holders, swimming with the racing tide, extol the "richness of the Internet" and recommend that it be made available to all schoolchildren. In truth, even middle-sized libraries have a richness of content and a diversity of entertainment and knowledge that dwarf the Internet and television combined.

I will support the library—that 100,000-channel medium.

15

Remote Storage

Remote, unfriended, melancholy, slow.

—Oliver Goldsmith, *The Traveller*

 After "budget cuts," there can be no two words more dismal than "remote storage." Libraries expand their collections in inexpansive buildings and, do what they will, have to deal with the huge gap between need and funding when it comes to new library buildings. In recent decades, academic and research libraries of all kinds have very often had to deal with both the need to preserve collections and the lack of available space. Remote storage is unappetizing even when compared to the shortcomings of alternatives. Compact shelving is very expensive to install in existing buildings and may not be possible in some. Library users, with good reason, hate microforms. Digitization is only a theoretical answer and likely to remain so. Weeding projects are, if done properly, very costly and it goes against the grain to spend so much money on a negative outcome. Yet still . . . remote storage sites are rarely custom-built and offer books substandard housing; the choice of volumes to be stored is immensely time and money consuming and, to put it mildly, inexact; remote collections cannot be browsed; much money has to be spent in maintaining the remote facility and in retrieving and delivering items. All in all, almost *anything* is preferable to remote storage.

> *I will seek every means I can to maximize the accessibility of my collections.*

16

Library of Congress Cards: R.I.P.

In the dull catalogue of common things . . .

—John Keats, *Lamia*

 The Library of Congress ceased to take orders for its catalogue cards on February 28, 1997. Sales had fallen from a high of seventy-eight million in 1968 (just before library automation really took off) to a touch more than half a million in 1996. LC began selling its cards at the turn of the century, so this great technological breakthrough and major force in twentieth-century librarianship lasted for nearly 100 years. There are still card catalogues, of course, in the places in which they always worked best—small libraries. It was a brilliant idea (first advanced thirty or more years before the first LC cards) to sell standardized sets of catalogue cards and to relieve libraries of much original cataloguing. The LC card was the force that gave us bibliographic standardization—because of the need for local cataloguing to be interfiled with LC's cataloguing—and a series of cataloguing codes that, essentially, taught us all LC practice. MARC was based on the LC card, and the card's legacy of the "main entry" still lives on in MARC and AACR2. It gave us a standard order for bibliographic data that is still found in catalogue codes and online catalogues.

Long after the LC card is only a distant memory for a few and unknown to most, its influence will linger and the good and the bad effects of that great enterprise will still be with us.

*I will think about the greatness of some
of our small artifacts in getting through
my daily routines.*

Two

Values

Islands in the Sea of Eternity

Beginning with the Vedas and the Bible, we
have welcomed the notion of sacred books.
In a certain way, every book is sacred.

—Jorge Luis Borges

 I once visited the Ryoan-ji Temple in Kyoto, Japan. That place of great beauty has, as one of its most famous sights, fifteen boulders of different sizes placed on a large oblong of immaculately white, precisely raked gravel. The "rock garden" is as timeless and elemental as the world itself and as modern as contemporary art. I asked, in my naive Occidental way, what the garden "meant" and was told by my gracious guides that the stones were said to symbolize a tigress leading her cubs across a river or islands in the sea of eternity. I tried to join the Japanese in their silent contemplation but all I could think of was "islands in the sea of eternity" and not the admirable tigress. Later, I thought about libraries and how they too are both timeless and modern. Libraries, in their vital role of preserving and making available the thoughts of humankind, can be said to be living islands in the sea of eternity—adrift in time, eternal, always dynamic.

I will contemplate the joyous path of libraries,
from the timeless to the timely.

Plain Words

Proper words in proper places, make the true definition of a style.

—Jonathan Swift, *Letter to a Young Clergyman*

 Our profession is, as is the rest of American life, beset with jargon and riddled with euphemism. Ernest Gowers wrote a guide to English for civil servants that later became a classic. It was called *Plain Words* (London, 1948) and was based on the notion that we should all aim for simplicity of expression, short declarative sentences, and, in general, writing what we mean to say and no more. I shudder to think what Sir Ernest would make of our modern professional literature. Many articles could be taken as examples of how not to write. Neologisms, computer jargon, management-speak, nouns transformed into verbs, and plain bad grammar abound in sentences that seem to go on forever. Library administrations issue memoranda that belong in the English Language Hall of Shame. Surely we librarians, of all people, should value clear, concise communication and the pleasures of words well written.

I will write clearly and value those who write clearly.

Intellectual Freedom

*If liberty means anything at all, it means
the right to tell people what they do not want
to hear.*

—George Orwell, from the
introduction to *Animal Farm*

 There are many reasons for a librarian to be a member
of the American Library Association, but if there were
no other, supporting ALA's Office for Intellectual
Freedom would be sufficient. Of all the values that define our
profession, surely one of the most important is the idea that
free expression of thought should be zealously protected in
libraries and by librarians. As many writers and thinkers have
observed, the test is the protection of expression with which
one does not agree. It is easy, after all, to defend expression of
ideas consonant with your own. It is the expression of the
minority, the despised, the different that we should protect at
all costs.

Our task is to preserve all the records of humanity, not
to pick and choose between those that suit our worldview and
those that do not. Ranganathan wrote that bad thought made
freely available is rendered sterile. There is nothing wrong
with librarians, particularly children's librarians, promoting the
uplifting and the life-enhancing. That is a far cry from sup-
pressing expression that you consider to be neither.

*I will strive to protect the intellectual
freedom of all.*

23

Privacy and the Library

Yet who could deny that privacy is a jewel?
It has always been the mark of privilege, the
distinguishing feature of a truly urbane culture.

—Phyllis McGinley, "In Defence of Sin,"
in *The Province of the Heart*

 The right to privacy is not spelled out in the Constitution of the United States. However, scholars and justices over many years have recognized it as an implicit constitutional right. It is now firmly entrenched within the law. Many applications of the right to privacy are far more sensational than the confidentiality of library records, but that confidentiality is a bond of trust between libraries and the people who use libraries. After all, the ability to be able to read or view whatever one wishes without interference or the knowledge of others is an important civil right. Book burning is characteristic of despotic regimes but thought control in the form of saying what one may read and the keeping of records of what one has read is much more common in such states. This is why library systems, particularly in this electronic age, should never keep records (or allow retrieval of records) of past library use by individuals. Also, the answer to requests for information on current library use should always be "where is your subpoena?"

I will guard and respect the confidentiality
of library records.

The Public Good

The noblest motive is the public good.

—Sir Richard Steele, *Spectator*

 So many surveys seem to be powerful engines for discovering the blindingly obvious. One recent example turned up the fact that two-thirds of those who do not use public libraries do not favor increasing taxes for libraries and would prefer a system of payment for use. Other surveys have shown the reluctance of some of the childless to pay taxes for schools and a reluctance to pay for, among other things, efficient mass transportation and a healthy environment.

Somewhere along the line, substantial numbers of people seem to have lost the notion that there is a general public good and that we should all pay for it according to our means and not only for such direct benefits that we derive. What we see is not just a fundamental difference of opinion, but a frightening shortsightedness. We need schools, parks, clean air and water, transportation systems, public libraries, and other manifestations of the public good because they benefit society, the economy, and the common culture. Not incidentally, they benefit each of us as individuals because they make our lives better, richer, and more enjoyable.

I will be an advocate for libraries as part of the public good.

Bibliotherapy

Books are not seldom talismans and spells.

—William Cowper,
The Task. vi. Winter Walk at Noon

 Bibliotherapy is the ancient practice of using books and reading in the treatment of the sick. Early on, bibliotherapy was closely tied to religion because the book most chosen to heal was the Bible. Later, physicians commonly prescribed reading as a therapeutic element for the emotionally ill and as a form of beneficial entertainment and instruction for those who were physically ill. Even those who are skeptical of bibliotherapy as such are aware from personal experience that reading can assuage troubles and calm the mind and spirit.

Hospitals have invariably had libraries of one sort or another. In the early twentieth century, enlightened hospitals hired librarians to work with physicians to treat the sick and great attention was paid to book selection and the recommendation of reading matter. Though it is not a major element of modern librarianship, bibliotherapy is still practiced and studied. There can be few librarians who have not experienced the healing power of books. Small wonder, then, that some of our pioneering colleagues have sought to extend that blessing to others.

I will value the therapy offered by books and reading.

The Reference Interview

. . . all questions are open.

—Clive Bell, *Civilisation*

 One of the least attractive ideas of those who think that technology is The Answer To Everything is "disintermediation." Lurking behind this ugly word is the idea that library users do not need librarians to help them find what they need in the library—machines can take care of that. Like most such ideas, it is not flat wrong but just the result of taking realities to illogical extremes. It is evident that online catalogs are used by many users with great effectiveness. On the other hand, most electronic searches of less organized or disorganized databases result in the user locating documents of marginal relevance rather than a comprehensive array of relevant documents. Any reference librarian will tell you that, more commonly than not, the question originally asked is a rough approximation of the question that the user really wants to ask. It is the special art of a good reference librarian to tease out the real needs of the library user and to match that question to the organized universe of knowledge. When it comes to reference work, no machine, no program, no "interactive system" comes even close to rivaling the skill of a trained human brain.

> *I will strive to be the best intermediary for library users.*

The Love of Books

*The library profession is . . . a profession
that is informed, illuminated, radiated by
a fierce and beautiful love of books. A love
so overwhelming that it engulfs community
after community and makes the culture of
our time distinctive, individual, creative,
and truly of the spirit.*

—Frances Clark Sayers, quoted in
The Reader's Quotation Book

 Some may find it hard to believe that, not so long ago,
the sentiments embodied in this quotation were the
commonly accepted coin of librarianship everywhere.
It should be noted that this fierce love of books was almost
never exclusionary and never denied the value of other forms
of communication. The history of libraries of all kinds tells us
that they have been eager and willing to incorporate other
media into their collections and services. From the beginning,
libraries have contained manuscripts, printed music, maps,
and objects such as coins, stamps, and artworks. In the last
century, we have added photographs, films, sound recordings,
and, recently, video recordings and electronic resources.

Each of these media has a place and each of them
should be catalogued, stored for access, and preserved to the
same degree as are books and journals. However, there is a
dangerous leveling tendency in those who say that books are
"just another medium of communication" and that computer
literacy is as important as real literacy—the ability to read and
write with proficiency. The truth is that reading is on a higher
intellectual plane and is a more worthwhile activity than, say,

viewing videos. Serious use of electronic resources leads to texts and those texts must be read. A computer printout is an inferior vehicle for reading but the process of reading and the level of literacy required are the same. There *is* something special about books and reading. We are right to love books not, in most cases, as objects but as the best medium for an activity that is at the heart of culture and society—reading.

> *I will accept no substitute for the unique value of books and reading.*

Small Libraries Are Beautiful

*Any intelligent fool can make things bigger,
more complex, and more violent. It takes a
touch of genius—and a lot of courage—to
move in the opposite direction.*

—E. F. Schumacher,
Small Is Beautiful

 It is my observation that the dominating factor in library user satisfaction is size. Just look at the libraries that most users love. Children's libraries, small public branch libraries, the one- or two-person departmental libraries in universities, special libraries in which the librarian works with the users as a colleague, private libraries. It is not difficult to see what makes these libraries special—the opportunity they afford for the librarians to get to know the users as people and the opportunity for those users to create a human relationship with the librarians and the library itself. Though huge libraries can inspire awe, it is very often the small library that inspires affection. In the end, it is the human scale and human relationships that count—in libraries as in the rest of life.

*I will maintain the humanity of small libraries
in libraries large and small.*

Clash of Values

Historians will have to face the fact that natural selection determined the evolution of cultures in the same manner as it did that of species.

—Konrad Lorenz, *On Aggression*

 Michael Frayn wrote that, socially, human beings are either carnivores or herbivores. Librarians evidently belong to the herbivorous tendency. Just look at our values—service, cooperation, intellectual freedom, and the Library Bill of Rights. Business, on the other hand, with its ethic of profit, competition, and the survival of the fittest is quintessentially carnivorous. For decades, the two worlds hardly overlapped or even knew much about each other. One way and another, our herbivorous Eden has been invaded by business values, practices, and corporate philosophies. The result is an uneasiness born of clashing values and mutually uncomprehending cultures.

It seems only yesterday that we learned "development" meant fund-raising; were introduced to strategic planning and all its trendy variants; and began to be governed by the stern discipline of the "bottom line." Librarians who would have died for "free service freely available to all" now contemplate fees for service with equanimity. Library administrators are not librarians but managers (in some cases by profession) and the gulf between the managers and the managed widens daily.

It was good that we adopted realism and efficiency but the process has gone too far; become too invasive. We

should cherish our enduring herbivorous values, place them far above commercial values, and use only those carnivorous ideas that make good library service more attainable.

I will not be devoured by the carnivorous style.

The Fear of Words

*Every person may freely speak, write, and
publish his or her sentiments on all subjects,
being responsible for the abuse of that right.*

—California State Constitution,
Article 1, section 2a

 Why do some people fear words and images? More
particularly, why do some Americans in this day and
age fear words and images to do with sex? People
who cheerfully tolerate hideous violence on TV or at the
movies seek to ban the likes of *Sex and Birth Control* from the
public library. This is by no means the most egregious example—that palm probably belongs to the effort to ban the
Merriam-Webster Collegiate Dictionary from the schools because
it defines "obscene" words. Words *are* powerful; images do stir
the mind and body but why the fear? Why are the banners
and censors, in the words of Laurence Peter, people who know
more than they think you ought to? (*Peter's Quotations*, 1977)
These questions are difficult to answer but surely the principle
is clear. Just as it is undemocratic to enforce reading, it is undemocratic to prevent reading. Librarians who are faced with challenges to books often feel—and are—isolated. All the more reason why we should show solidarity and proclaim the right of
our users to have unfettered access to all lawful publications.

*I will stand with our sisters and brothers in
defense of intellectual freedom against officious
and fearful Bumbledom.*

"Non Omnis Moriar"

I have created a monument longer lasting than bronze.
—Horace, Ars Poetica

 Horace wrote "I shall not altogether die." Nor will he as long as his words are preserved and read. This is a weighty responsibility for librarians—our duty to preserve the knowledge of the past and present for the people of the future. Each advance in human communication is less durable than its predecessor but more numerous and easily transported. We have "progressed" from words on "everlasting bronze" (Horace again) to words transmitted around the world in the twinkling of an eye and lost forever just as swiftly. I have read that one-quarter of all feature films ever made have been lost. No one knows how durable CDs, for example, will prove to be and the short history of digital storage is replete with examples of knowledge and information lost forever. Only a minute fraction of texts printed in books has ever been lost and perhaps it is through multiple copies of books printed on permanent paper that we can best fulfill our mission.

I will value books for their content and for their role in preserving knowledge.

Three

Lives

Mister Jones

He was a good man and a just.

—Gospel of St. Luke, 23:50

He was about sixty-five then and had joined the library before 1914—the year he went off to war. He was quite deaf and his attempts to guess partly heard questions sometimes produced baffling answers. He liked and cared about the people who used that small library and would often keep newly arrived books for people he knew. "She'll like that one," he'd say and surely she did. "The readers are always right," he'd say and I have always tried to remember that. Of course, they were "readers" then and not "patrons" but it really is the same. Mr. Jones always dressed correctly and had a courtly and considerate way about him. With all his shortcomings, the readers responded to his civility and willingness to serve. What good would the keenest intellect and the sharpest hearing be without these qualities?

I will remember that service is more than simply expertise.

Teaching by Helping

There is no such whetstone, to sharpen a good wit and encourage a will to learning, as is praise.

—Roger Ascham, *The Schoolmaster*

 One of the wisest librarians I have ever known said "an ounce of help is worth a ton of instruction." Surely it is true that the vast majority of people seek assistance in libraries rather than to be taught. Library instruction is a necessary and important fact of modern academic library life but it should always be directed to empowering the students to help themselves and to know when and how they should seek help from librarians. The important thing is to create a climate in which even the shyest person feels able to ask for help without being judged inadequate. Good librarians are not only able to give assistance but are also people who welcome and even seek the questions that are the first step on the ladder of knowledge.

I will empower, not overwhelm, the learner.

S. R. Ranganathan (1892–1972)

> *Lives of great men all remind us*
> *We can make our lives sublime.*
>
> —H. W. Longfellow, *The Psalm of Life*

 Shiyali Ramamrita Ranganathan was, by common consent, the great librarian of the twentieth century. He rivals Melvil Dewey—the giant of nineteenth-century librarianship—in the range of his interests, the depths and variety of his contributions to librarianship, and the originality of his thought. He began adult life as a mathematician but his career changed when, at the age of thirty-two, he was appointed Librarian of the University of Madras. Unlike most academics transported into such a position, he took his responsibilities seriously enough to go to library school at University College, London. One of the things of which I am most proud is that I can claim a link to Ranganathan as a Fellow of the (British) Library Association.

Although he is most noted for his groundbreaking work in the field of classification and his seminal *Five Laws of Library Science,* Ranganathan wrote about and influenced almost all fields of librarianship. His was a major influence in the revolution in descriptive cataloguing that culminated in *AACR2*. He was a leader in the field of national bibliography, the person who inspired the development of libraries in post-colonial India, and a leading figure in international librarianship. There is a sense of greatness and nobility of soul in all the many reminiscences of Dr. Ranganathan. Above all, he was an

idealist who saw librarianship as a vital tool in the development of humankind and a day coming when our profession would play a part in achieving universal peace.

I will rejoice in the achievements of great librarians.

Libraries in Literature

> *. . . the great main building of the Public Library, a building filled with books and unimaginably vast, and which he had never dared yet to enter . . . he had never gone in because the building was so big that it must be full of corridors and marble steps, in the maze of which he would be lost and never find the book he wanted.*
>
> —James Baldwin, *Go Tell It on the Mountain*

 The excellent anthology *Reading Rooms* (Doubleday, 1991) is a celebration of public libraries in American literature. A comprehensive collection of literary writings on libraries from all countries and eras would itself occupy a small library because literature is full of libraries. There are great libraries, such as that which frightened the young James Baldwin, and small libraries, such as those celebrated in what seems like every other autobiographical novel. There are marble halls and one-room libraries and the collections cherished in each. Dreams are born in these literary libraries and meetings take place between eccentrics, lovers, the studious, and the desperate. There is youth in the literary works of older people remembering visions and far-off lands they found in books when they were children. There is age and wisdom in the celebration of a lifetime of reading and library use. There are also librarians of all sorts in literature—scary librarians and kind librarians, fussy librarians and learned librarians.

> *I will take pride in the rich literary life of libraries.*

Hugh Craig Atkinson (1933–1986)

I have studied the lives of great men and famous women; and I found that the men and women who got to the top were those that did the jobs they had in hand with everything they had of energy, enthusiasm, and hard work.

—Harry S. Truman, quoted in
The Book of Unusual Quotations

 Hugh Atkinson was a great librarian by Harry Truman's definition or any other. He worked in a number of major academic libraries, notably as the University Librarian at, successively, Ohio State and the University of Illinois (he referred to both great research institutions, in inimitably Atkinsonian manner, as "cow colleges"). I had the privilege of working with him in the last nine years of his cruelly shortened life and to this day consult my memories of him and his words on all important library matters. He had an unbeatable combination of knowledge, experience, and flair combined with more personality than it is fair for any one person to possess. He shaped his libraries for the better; loved library collections *and* library technology; made service to all library users the touchstone of all programs and decisions; mixed common sense with a powerful intellect that he tried to mask in plain, and often earthy, language; and inspired and enriched the lives of his colleagues. Hugh was unique. I miss him every day of my professional life and would feel blessed if I were ever half the librarian he was.

I will draw inspiration from the work of librarians I have known.

Pity the Poor Administrator

*Work is accomplished by those employees who
have not yet reached their level of incompetence.*

—Lawrence J. Peter and Raymond Hull,
The Peter Principle

 I have worked on many levels (from the lowest up) in
many different libraries for too many years. For most
of the last two decades, I have been an administrator.
I am one of the class of such persons that worries constantly
about being a living example of the Peter Principle and has the
occasional pang of guilt over the level of compensation. (The
other class is that of the sublime egotists.) I am told that it is
best to be "in charge." Perhaps, but I am not sure any library
administrator has had that experience. That is not solely
because, no matter how high you climb, there is always someone above. It is also because societal changes and justice
demand that one has to persuade others in order to accomplish anything. The day of the library autocrat is long over and
I wistfully wonder if *anything* that I particularly want ever
comes to pass in the library!

The standard excuse for us being paid more is a combination of experience and "the burdens of office." My private
justification is that, as one rises, the level of fun sinks. Believe
me, I was much happier cataloguing all day than I am attend-
ing lengthy, dreary, unproductive meetings or attempting to
adjudicate personnel disputes. I must not complain too much.
At least in a medium-sized or small library the director has

some contact with real library issues. In large libraries, the work life of the director is indistinguishable from that of the CEO of Acme Widgets, Inc.

> *I will try to find a balance between competence and job satisfaction.*

Andrew Carnegie (1835–1919)

*[The Salvation Army] . . . would take money
from the Devil himself and be only too glad to
get it out of his hands and into God's.*

—George Bernard Shaw, preface to *Major Barbara*

 Andrew Carnegie must, surely, be one of history's
clearest examples of duality of character. Carnegie
moved to America at the age of ten when his father, a
Scottish weaver, lost his business to mechanization. He started
work at thirteen and rose from the lowliest of positions to
become one of the richest men in the world. Creator and
owner of Carnegie Steel, he could exhibit a ruthlessness and
human indifference that was remarkable even in that rapa-
cious, indifferent age. Carnegie exploited his workers, employed strike breakers and spies to break unions, polluted and
despoiled the landscape, and used his genius for business with
no observable scruples.

Then, at the age of sixty-six, Carnegie sold his empire
for half a billion dollars and devoted the rest of his life to good
works and the search for peace. His philanthropy paid for
more than 2,500 library buildings worldwide (1,679 public
and 108 university libraries in the United States) and supported
many other good educational and social causes. He set out his
principles in the *Gospel of Wealth,* which demands philanthropy from the rich, though not in the amassing of their
money. We are faced with the moral paradox of money gained
in disreputable ways being used in support of genuinely good

causes—libraries chief among them. How can we reconcile the two sides of such a life—the malefactor of great wealth and the deeply religious benefactor of humanity? Perhaps charity as penance is better than no penance at all.

I will weigh the source of library philanthropy against its benefits.

What Do You Remember from Library School?

Nostalgia isn't what it used to be.

—Graffito, noted in *The Penguin Dictionary of Modern Quotations*

 Some people remember their library school with fondness, some as a necessary but tedious step to get their "union card." In my experience the fondness increases as the years advance and the time in library school recedes. I left library school some thirty years ago; one of the two teachers who influenced me most began the year I enrolled and has been retired for some time. I remember that period and, especially, the people with affection.

It is interesting to ask librarians what they remember about library school. The vast majority will talk more about their teachers and fellow students than about specific topics and will remember best the inspiration that a teacher provided rather than the knowledge that she or he imparted. It has been said that a teacher gives knowledge and a guru enlightenment. For many of us, it is that enlightenment, that sense of truly understanding some aspect of librarianship for the first time, that is the most vivid memory of library school.

I will enlighten people about librarianship.

47

Melvil Dewey (1851–1931)

*The genius bears the full weight of what
is common and exists hundreds and thousands
of times over.*

—John Berger, *A Painter of Our Time*

 Melvil Louis Kossuth Dewey was a protean genius. It is only a mild exaggeration to say that he, in the last quarter of the nineteenth century, invented and established modern librarianship in the teeth of opposition and almost single-handedly. Consider for a moment the achievements for which he is renowned. He drove the formation of the American Library Association, founded the *Library Journal* and the Library Bureau, and published the first edition of his *Decimal Classification*—all in 1876 when he was twenty-five years old! He is the father of modern classification theory and practice; the father of the modern library school (though he can scarcely be blamed for their contemporary transmutations); an early and ardent advocate of standardization, mechanization, and cost efficiency in librarianship; the person who established (at Columbia University) the exemplar of the great centralized research library; and the founder (through his work as New York State Librarian) of the modern state library concept. Biographers, while lauding his achievements, have noted impatience, his desire for power, occasional abrasiveness, fondness for females, and obsession with spelling reform. Be all that as it may, Dewey was a doer and a prophet, a maker and an idealist, a hard-working, driven man who saw farther

than anyone else in his field and had the character and ability to accomplish what he dreamed.

> *I will build on the energy, accomplishments, and ideals of the founders of modern librarianship.*

Lonely People

The unimaginable lodge
For solitary thinkings.

—John Keats, *Endymion*

 Working in a library teaches you that there are a lot of lonely people in the world and, to many of them, the library is a source of solace. Most public libraries provide a warm, comfortable place that asks no questions and demands nothing beyond ordinary decorum of those who frequent it. The library of a college or university is one of the few places on campus in which lonely students can spend time in the presence of others without stress or having to "fit in." There are many stories of solitary children finding peace of mind in the school library. It seems that a number of lonely people actually make new friends in libraries and many more appreciate the humanity of the library's staff. All libraries have their "regulars" and, as one gets to know them a little, it often becomes obvious that the library makes up for an absence in their lives, that books and other materials are a source of consolation as well as knowledge, and that friendliness and helpfulness in the staff are as prized as expertise. It may not be *the* reason for libraries to exist but the fact that we make lonely lives less lonely is no mean contribution to society.

I will do what I can to make my library
a compassionate place.

50

Miss Colwell

She can teach ye how to climb.

—John Milton, *Comus*

 I was eight when I moved with my family to Hendon—a North London suburb. The children's library, on the left just after you entered the stately central library, became my second home and daily resort. As well as all the authors that I loved and came to love, that library had all manner of wonderful things—story hours; silver and (better) gold stars for reading; the chance to be a "book monitor" and actually be behind The Desk. This marvelous place was presided over by a "lady" known, with some awe, as "Miss Colwell." As children do, I took the library and her for granted. Many years later, in library school, I discovered that she was Eileen Colwell—the doyenne of British children's librarianship who had, literally, written the book on the subject. All unknowing, I had met my first Great Library Person! The people who think themselves lions of our profession are often noisy and showy while the truly great are content to serve in the shade.

I will keep, as part of me, the librarians
who shaped my own life.

Retirement

. . . they rest from their labours, and their
works do follow them.

—Revelation 14:11

 I attended my first retirement party when I was very young and had been working in my first library for only a few months. A gentleman was retiring after having worked in the same small public library system for more than forty years. Amid the presents and the congratulations, the cakes and the cups of tea, he talked about the old days, of colleagues long gone, of how the library had grown, and made little jokes about who would be doing his duties and who would keep the young people up to the mark. Later, he took his few remaining personal possessions and his gifts, said goodnight, and left at his usual time.

Retirement seemed a distant, unimaginable state to me then but I remember thinking about the huge change that was taking place in his life and what retirees left behind—the accumulation of collections built, service rendered, and relationships sustained. Even for the most dedicated, work should not be the most important thing in life, but it is an important facet of a life and its ending should be marked appropriately. We need to do more to honor lifetimes of work than we do in often perfunctory retirement ceremonies of platitudes and gifts. We should honor the good that people have done because years of work matter for years after they are over.

I will value the gifts my longtime colleagues
leave when they move on.

Four

Laws

Ranganathan's Five Laws

*. . . I shall certainly admit a system as
empirical or scientific only if it is capable
of being tested by experience.*

—Karl Popper, *The Logic of Scientific Discovery*

 S. R. Ranganathan invented the term *library science*. He believed that all human activities were susceptible to analysis using the scientific method and that such a careful examination of the phenomena of library work could lead to the formulation of empirical "laws." His are clearly not laws in the sense that, say, the Second Law of Thermodynamics is a law. However, they are more than mere generalities because they are founded on observation and analysis by a trained mind. (Dr. Ranganathan was originally a mathematician.) He, like that other genius of librarianship, Melvil Dewey, used high intelligence, the scientific approach, and considerable experience in his rethinking of our profession.

Ranganathan's Five Laws of Library Science:

> Books are for use
>
> Every book its reader
>
> Every reader his book
>
> Save the time of the reader
>
> The library is a growing organism

*I will know Ranganathan's laws to better
understand my work.*

Ranganathan's First Law

Books are for use.

—S. R. Ranganathan,
The Five Laws of Library Science

 One of the astounding things about Dr. Ranganathan's Five Laws is the depth of meaning compressed into so few words. Such concision is characteristic of Western poetry and Eastern teaching (secular and spiritual). Even in Ranganathan's day, books were not the only documents collected by libraries, and it is wrong to conclude from his words that books were the only library materials that mattered to Ranganathan. His essential point is that libraries acquire materials and make them accessible so they can be *used.* This is the real difference between libraries and museums. With few exceptions, books and other library materials are important not as objects but for the knowledge and information they contain. Even the maintenance of unused or little-used items in research libraries must be justified in terms of potential use. For most collections in most libraries, we must heed this law and value usefulness above all else.

*I will build collections not for vanity
but for use.*

Ranganathan's Second Law

Every book its reader.

—S. R. Ranganathan,
The Five Laws of Library Science

 Let me first update the terminology of this law. "Every item of library material its user" lacks the snap of Dr. Ranganathan's formulation but expresses modern reality better. This law teaches us two lessons. The first is that we do not acquire library materials in the abstract. Each acquisition should call to mind a potential user—by name (if something has been requested specifically) or by type. Both general and specific collection decisions are, of course, dictated by knowledge of the community the library serves. One must base decisions not only on the known community of the present but also on likely future changes in that community. The second lesson is that even the most apt selection choices can be vitiated if they are not backed up by an efficient and user-friendly bibliographic control system. The law works both ways. Acquire only those things with potential to be used and ensure that library users can speedily and accurately locate the very material that they wish to use.

> *I will add useful items to the collection
> and make them accessible to all.*

Ranganathan's Third Law

Every reader his book.

—S. R. Ranganathan,
The Five Laws of Library Science

 This law is the complementary reverse of its predecessor. As with the other laws, we need to see beyond the words to the meaning they embody. Dr. Ranganathan certainly did not mean to imply that all "readers" (library users) are male or that only males are governed by this precept. Nor, again, did he mean that books are the only useful library materials. He did believe that reading is a most important path to learning and wisdom—a sometimes unfashionable view among the false egalitarians of today who proclaim that viewing images or manipulating computer data is the intellectual equivalent of the sustained reading of text. Leaving that aside, Ranganathan is telling us that when a library user comes to a library or gains access to library services, certain materials (textual, graphic, and/or numeric) will meet her or his needs. It is our job to ensure that the connection between Library User A and Materials B is made and that connection is as speedy and practical as possible. That is why we select useful materials, create usable catalogues, provide helpful reference service, and do all the other things that add up to total library service. Another lesson is to be found in the words "every reader." We should never forget that every single member of the community we serve is entitled to access to all our collections and to the very best service we can provide.

*I will be the connection between the users
of my library and the materials they need.*

58

Ranganathan's Fourth Law

Save the time of the reader.

—S. R. Ranganathan,
The Five Laws of Library Science

 I have known libraries in which the policies and procedures seemed to be designed primarily for the benefit of library staff and administrators. In such cases, good, service-oriented librarians and staff are often hobbled in their ability to serve and benefit library users. Ranganathan's fourth law is, when properly understood and employed, a management tool of great utility. A library that examined every aspect of its policies, rules, procedures, or systems with that one simple criterion in mind—saving the time of the library users—would find the consequent changes transformational. This is a more complicated process than it might appear. Consider these questions. Would self-charging be quicker for the library user than an efficiently run, well-staffed circulation desk? Imagine a good service-oriented supermarket. Few would think that its service would be enhanced if we had to wand and pack our own groceries. How can you run a reference desk to deliver speedier and better service without setting up potentially cumbersome queuing systems for in-depth reference service, informational questions, and telephone enquiries? Does the speed and ease of use of academic departmental libraries outweigh their undoubted inefficiencies and expensive labor-intensiveness? Frugality with the time of others must be paramount in our decision-making process.

> *I will always bear in mind that the time of library users is precious.*

Ranganathan's Fifth Law

The library is a growing organism.

—S. R. Ranganathan,
The Five Laws of Library Science

 The new British Library building in London is merely the largest and the latest of the many examples of the perils of ignoring this law. Thirty years plus in the planning, it was full the day it opened. Libraries do grow and change and will always do so. Compact shelving, microforms, and electronic resources might seem to imply less growth or even shrinkage, but there is no evidence that is so. Space continues to be at a premium in most libraries. To offer but one example, the ubiquity of computers in modern libraries has placed more demands on our space and infrastructure. A computer workstation and its peripherals take up far more space than a place for a person to sit to read and take notes. Books, journals, videos, and sound recordings continue to be published in great numbers, and the slowdown in the growth of many collections has been caused by financial constraints and not the availability of, or demand for, new materials. Change comes along with growth and healthy growth implies flexibility in the use of space, the deployment of staff, and the nature or our programs.

> *I will remember that libraries grow and*
> *develop and will plan accordingly.*

Five New Laws of Librarianship

Small people on the shoulders of giants see farther than the giants themselves.

—Stella Didacus (Diego de Estella)

 Ranganathan's Five Laws underlie my beliefs and work as a librarian. His shadow fell hugely on my library education and his influence pervaded almost all the classes I took. (One particularly enthusiastic teacher had set the Five Laws to music!) Ranganathan's work and, particularly, the twenty-four words of the *Laws,* provided an intellectual framework for understanding all aspects of library work. It was the force behind the two most precious things we gained from library school—enthusiasm and insight. (I sometimes wonder if contemporary library education with its emphasis on technology and "information"—can have the same beneficial results.) Given my reverence for Ranganathan, it was a potentially hubristic act to create five new laws of librarianship—not with the intent of replacing his Laws but as an experiment in analyzing our situation today in the light of his ideas. My new laws:

> Libraries serve humanity
>
> Respect all forms by which knowledge is communicated
>
> Use technology intelligently to enhance service
>
> Protect free access to knowledge
>
> Honor the past and create the future

I will apply fundamental principles to guide me through new situations.

First New Law
Libraries serve humanity

Freely we serve
Because we freely love, as in our will
To love or not; in this we stand or fall.

—John Milton, *Paradise Lost*

 Libraries are about service or they are about nothing. In everything we do, from an individual act of assistance to a library user to our collective efforts to support education and preserve knowledge for posterity, we are animated by the will to serve. What motivates the altruism, the commitment to serve, that is present in all good librarians? Not material gain or fame—librarians are overblessed with neither. There are gains, though, in successful service; psychic rewards that cannot be quantified but are no less real for that. We get those rewards daily by giving benefits to library users and the wider community; by serving individuals and serving humankind. Before we can deliver and reap the rewards of service, we must identify the benefits that society can reasonably expect and then devise means of delivering those benefits. Service always has a purpose, and our careers of service have a purpose. They are neither menial nor small. It is hard to imagine a more worthy or nobler role in life.

I will derive my reward from service
to humanity.

Second New Law
Respect all forms by which knowledge is communicated

*Being poor and unable to afford the amenities
of wealthier Americans, I thank the public
library for giving me an opportunity to enjoy
the world of video . . . using my library card
has made my life fuller and better . . .*

—Bill Pease (Tacoma, Washington),
quoted in the ALA national campaign
Libraries Change Lives

 I value the electronic resources that are available in my library. I enjoy using them to locate texts and images to read and view. I look forward to the day when access to these resources is less hit-and-miss and we have reached a resolution of the difficult issues that surround them—preservation of electronic records, intellectual property, provenance, etc. When that happy day dawns, and if it is in my lifetime, I will continue to use and enjoy using sound recordings and videos and reading magazines and books.

We all, consciously or not, use different means of communication for the special value they bring to our pursuit of knowledge, information, and entertainment. Put simply, those of us privileged to have access to electronic resources use the Net to locate images, data, and brief texts, and we use books, sound recordings, videos, etc., for study and entertainment. We know in our hearts that the power of print-on-paper

to convey recorded knowledge in lengthy texts is unrivaled and will remain so. Is there a more absurd question than "which should be supported, books or bytes"? Surely not. We should value all means of preserving and communicating the records and achievements of the human mind and heart.

> *I will resist pressure to deny one useful format to patrons, in favor of another.*

Third New Law
Use technology intelligently to enhance service

The technology of medicine has outgrown its sociology.

—Henry Sigerist, *Medicine and Human Welfare*

 Technology, intelligently applied, is a wonderful life-enhancing thing. The telephone was an almost unalloyed boon until the advent of dinner-hour telephone solicitation and restaurant diners making and receiving calls on cellular telephones. Similarly, the online catalogue, now transformed into the all-singing, all-dancing online system, changed almost every aspect of librarianship for the better. Now, we have moved on from these wondrous systems to a point at which the construction of Web pages has become a consuming obsession in library schools and some libraries. It is as though we have taken useful tools and, like so many Sorcerer's Apprentices, caused them to run riot, dominate our libraries, and devastate our budgets. Does every employee in the library really need access to a powerful personal computer? It seems to be accepted that they do, even when the PC's main function is that of an electronic gathering place that has replaced the watercooler as the venue for nonwork discussions. Technology exists to support our mission as librarians, to assist in ready and free access to recorded knowledge and

information, and to deliver library service effectively. Anything beyond that is the path to dashed expectations and skewed priorities.

> *I will use technology when it is useful,*
> *affordable, and cost-effective.*

Fourth New Law
Protect free access to knowledge

*There are two good things in life—freedom
of thought and freedom of action.*

—W. Somerset Maugham, *Of Human Bondage*

 Almost all librarians oppose censorship, resist the book burners and banners, and defend the First Amendment. Some, though, fail to understand the more insidious threat to intellectual freedom the "virtual library" represents. This may seem paradoxical, since the priests of technology preach of a coming age in which everyone is a publisher and the freedom to propagate and receive ideas is unlimited. Reality is very different.

To begin with, the Internet is by no means "free," is laboring under a level of use that it was not designed to bear, and is already subject to censorship. We will soon see restrictions on access to the Net, high individual charges for that access, and monitoring of its use. Moreover, that future concerns only those with means of access. The most inflated number of those on the Net is 20 million (the number of regular, active users being much smaller). What of the other 240 million Americans? What of the uncounted millions in other countries (many of which lack regular power supply)?

The virtual library is a profoundly elitist concept, dreamed up by academics, that would exclude the bulk of

67

Americans and the masses of people throughout the world. Do we really want a small, prosperous, knowledgeable overclass dominating a huge, illiterate underclass? Tyrants have burned books but they could not burn all the copies. The tyranny of the electronic elite would be far more efficient.

> *I will use technology to support and increase free access to knowledge, not to deny it to the world's have-nots.*

Fifth New Law
Honor the past and create the future

Time present and time past
Are both perhaps present in time future
And time future contained in time past.

—T. S. Eliot, *Burnt Norton*

 Two characters emerge in the current discussion on the future of libraries: nostalgists who loathe electronic technology and anything more modern than the printing press, and technophiles who scorn all the past—including last year's computer. Surely there must be a few benighted souls who fit in each category, but rational discourse is about balance and the rate of possible change. Rational people discuss the balance in present and future libraries between print, video, or sound recordings on the one hand, and electronic texts, images, and databases on the other. Rational people recognize that each medium of communication has its strengths, weaknesses, and role to play. Rational people look at the reality of library use, library collections, and library services and project from that. Extremists dream a future and make assertions that have no basis in reality or common sense. Old things are not valuable because they are old, but valuable old things must continue. New things are neither good nor bad because they are new, but must be evaluated on their costs and usefulness. Wise people will understand the past of libraries, know why they are what they are today, and build a future based on tradition and innovation.

I will give library users what they want—
balance between the old and the new.

69

Five

Change, Problems, & Realities

Change Makes You Stupid

With the only certainty in our daily existence being change, and the rate of change growing always faster in a kind of technological leapfrog game, speed helps people to think they are keeping up.

—Gail Sheehy, *Speed Is of the Essence*

 I once heard a speaker say "Change makes you stupid," a dramatic way of making the point that we gain experience and knowledge in a job over the years and then the job changes. Bingo!—all that experience and knowledge count for nothing. There are two types of change in the workplace. Bad change is a result of a decision that a useful product or service should be axed purely to save money. Libraries are not immune from such bad change. The other kind is a change in the method of achieving a worthwhile goal. This may have bad individual consequences, as in the case of the loss of manual and other unskilled jobs to technology. Continuing individual tragedies exist because society has not found a way to meet the need for training and education that would avert them. On the whole, changes in method are good and should be welcomed by those who work in libraries when they result in better service to library users.

I will welcome service-oriented change and encourage retraining of those displaced by it.

Outsourcing

*One of our defects as a nation is a tendency
to use what have been called "weasel words."*

—Theodore Roosevelt, in a 1916 speech

 Ugly words often bespeak ugly actions. The wise librarian has learned to distrust management-speak— the language that always conceals an attempt to save money by diminishing the quality of work life and service. Outsourcing is a practice in industry of contracting for things to be made or services rendered by outside companies. It has crept into the public sector including, alas, libraries. The crucial distinction should be between tasks that require professional or technical expertise and knowledge of the local library and its programs and those that do not. In other words, a move to outsource photocopying or janitorial services is, all things being equal, acceptable. Outsourcing cataloguing, selection, and acquisitions is not. The managers who make such decisions are saying, in effect, that professional library skills and experience can be replaced by distant vendors who probably lack the former and certainly lack the latter. Not only are "outsourced" catalogues and collections bad policy because of their inevitable debasement of service, they also attack the very foundations of our profession.

*I will take pride in my professional skills
and resist attempts to debase them.*

Scholarly Journals

Specialist—A man who knows more and more about less and less.

—William J. Mayo, quoted in
Cassell's Book of Humorous Quotations

 The scholarly journal is a phenomenon with an odd history and an uncertain future. Its impact on academic libraries has been profound and, for the most part, misunderstood. More than 200 years ago, the first journals covered all aspects of the sciences, arts, and life and were published for the wealthy with intellectual curiosity, a liberal education, and time on their hands. The scholarly journal of today could not be more different. It has dwindled to a form in which knowledge is fragmented into an endless number of sub-sub-specialties. The result has been great expense for libraries and consequent calls for revolutionary change. Most scholarly journals have hundreds of authors and tens of readers, if that. A large number of their articles go uncited and, presumably, unread. Most people believe that the prices of all journals increase at an unconscionable rate. In fact, at one extreme, arts and humanities journals are moderately priced and their prices grow slowly. At the other extreme we find the real villains—scientific, medical, and technical journals— grossly overpriced to begin with and subject to volatile annual increases. If these journals were to be switched from paper to electronic distribution, we would take a giant step to save the academic library from their depredations.

I will not accept the high-priced serial syndrome as inevitable or unalterable.

Foreign Languages

Languages are the pedigrees of nations.

—Samuel Johnson, quoted in
James Boswell's *A Tour of the Hebrides*

 Up to now, Americans have been, by and large, mono-lingual. This is only to be expected in the world's only superpower and a country whose language is spoken throughout the world. In the past, relatively few librarians needed foreign languages. Those who did were engaged in cataloguing, special collections work, and other esoterica. As America becomes more and more ethnically and linguistically diverse, however, language skills have moved out of the back rooms and into the frontline of direct public service. Huge areas of this country have at least a substantial minority of Spanish-speaking inhabitants, and other languages, spoken by young and old, predominate elsewhere. I have seen an adver-tisement for a library position in Florida that was entirely in Spanish—a sure harbinger of a marketplace for librarians with language skills. Librarians who wish to serve the diverse soci-ety of twenty-first-century America would be well advised to learn a second language not, as in the past, to be a specialist but to broaden the range of their career possibilities.

> *I will learn something of other languages
> to help me communicate with all the
> library's users.*

Modern Library Budgets

 Many younger librarians have known nothing but reactive budgets—the kind in which the fight is to preserve what you have, in which you count it a victory if the cuts are smaller than expected. Even in good times, library budgets are constrained by many forces—the inflexibility and relative size of our personnel budgets; annual excessive increases in the price of our materials; the need to purchase more electronic resources and hardware while maintaining book and journal collections; uncontrollable costs such as postage and telecommunications; the fact that the capital budget is usually not the library's to control.

Even given all that, it is still possible to see our budgets as priorities expressed numerically. The wise librarian budgets to cut equally—to spread the pain across all programs and services—but budgets to grow unequally. Any opportunity for financial growth, no matter how small, should be seized as an opportunity to fund a priority, and not to increase everything by a minute amount. Those numbers in the budget should be every bit as much an expression of what is important to the library as the most eloquent essay.

*I will decide what is important to the library
and seek funding for it.*

The Newbery Medal

You must write for children as you do for adults, only better.

—Attributed to Maxim Gorky,
The Penguin Dictionary of Modern Quotations

 I have always thought that one of the hardest and simultaneously most enjoyable tasks in our profession would be to be a member of the Newbery Medal committee. Since 1922, dedicated members of what is now the Association for Library Service to Children (ALSC) have read all the year's children's titles in search of the best of the best. There is a great diversity of writing for children, great differences in the age ranges of the intended audience, and enormous increases in the quantity and quality (physically and in content) of children's books. Given all that, the Newbery committee faces a daunting task each year—one that makes choosing the Champion at the Westminster Dog Show look laughably easy. The unique cachet of the Newbery Medal and its acceptance as "the children's Pulitzer" by parents, teachers, and children themselves is a tribute to the hard work and professionalism of our colleagues. Looking back, there are a few winners of the Medal that seem less than worthy, but then fashions and times change. Overall, the Newbery Medal is a shining example of excellence sought and found.

I will delight in the wealth of children's literature and honor my colleagues in that field.

Books into Films

*If my books had been any worse, I would not
have been invited to Hollywood, and if they
had been any better, I should not have come.*

—Raymond Chandler, quoted in
Frank McShane's *The Life of Raymond Chandler*

 Many of the different media that libraries contain are
related—audio books, art books, sound recordings
and scores, etc.—but none have such a paradoxical
relationship as books and films. Movies are pale shadows of
great books, but some great movies have been made from sec-
ond-rate books. The greater the literature, the more likely it is
to teem with too much life to be captured by even the longest
film. A literary depiction of the human condition depends on
the interaction of reader and words, not on simple description
or action. Poems, which contain the maximum of meaning in
the minimum of words, are unfilmable by definition.
Contrariwise, genre novels (romances, Westerns, spy thrillers,
etc.) are eminently filmable because of their strong narratives
and plenty of action. There are great novels that have strong
stories amid much more—the resulting films have all the story
and little of the insight. Libraries, of course, value both books
and the movies based on them because they are equally used.
We should remember, though, that masterpieces of the cine-
ma are independent works with their own qualities—few of
which overlap with those of great literature.

*I will recommend reading the book, even
if they have seen the movie.*

Burnout

No better. No worse. No change.

—Samuel Beckett, *Happy Days*

 "Burnout" is variously supposed to derive from astrophysics, electrical engineering, the drug culture, and Graham Greene's *A Burnt-Out Case*. Whatever its origins, this compelling metaphor speaks to us of a peculiarly modern condition produced when boredom meets despair, when alienation and incapacity to function are complete, when the accumulation of experience is more than the soul can bear. It seems almost too dramatic a state to be produced by library work, but it can and does happen to us and its consequences are many and dire.

Burnout comes when cataloguing ceases to be a pleasure and a puzzle and becomes drudgery; when delivering the same library instruction class and answering the same reference questions over and over again become intolerable; when just going to work causes numbness or dread. Repetition is an obvious contributing factor, as is having to accomplish more and more with fewer and fewer resources, as is the feeling that the work is mounting and nothing worthwhile is being accomplished.

We should all remember that the sense of being valued is an antidote to burnout—value our own work and extend the courtesy of appreciation to our colleagues.

I will help my colleagues avoid burnout and be alert to the signs of burnout in myself.

Reference Collections

Dictionaries are like watches; the worst is better than none, and the best cannot be expected to go quite true.

—Samuel Johnson, quoted in *Johnsoniana*

 I have always been fascinated by reference books though I would be hard put to define the term. Perhaps the only valid definition is . . . a book that is in the reference library. Dictionaries, almanacs, encyclopedias, gazetteers, and directories are clearly designed for reference use—their arrangement, typography, elaborate indexes bespeak their purpose. Nevertheless, libraries have some dictionaries in the general collection and books less obviously for reference in the reference collection. The truth is that most reference collections are shaped around the needs of the library users as expressed in reference questions. All electronic resources are, of course, potential reference tools. Their great strength lies in the ability of the online user to isolate a fact, image, factoid, or short passage from within large databases and lengthy texts and use it to answer reference questions and other pleas for help. If you take a reference text and digitize it, you are making it more useful because all the carefully assembled structure facilitates electronic searching. But there's the rub. The internal guideposts and careful construction of reference materials are not present in other texts, and research then degenerates into the inefficiencies and noise of keyword searching.

I will not try to make silk reference work out of a sow's free-text search.

Distant Learning

'Tis distance lends enchantment to the view
And robes the mountain in its azure haze.

—Thomas Campbell, *Pleasures of Hope*

 One of the most seductive prospects in higher education is ungrammatically named "distance learning." The idea is that students in remote places will be able, by means of two-way interactive communication technology, to receive an education via "virtual classrooms" conducted by teachers of the highest caliber. Three classes of people—politicians, administrators, and technology boosters—are hyping distant learning as education without the expense of new campuses, classroom buildings, or libraries. Two classes of people—teachers and librarians—have some well-founded reservations.

Teachers fear that nothing can replace the human interaction between teacher and student inside or outside the classroom. They also fear that technology will mechanize and cheapen the educational process and pedagogy will dwindle to the provision of canned videos. Librarians point out that, almost by definition, the distant learner is one without access to adequate library resources and services. Though we can supply some materials by fax and interlibrary loan, and though some materials are available electronically, none of these come even close to the educational experience afforded by access to comprehensive library collections and services. If distant learning is to be successful, it must be as a supplement not an alternative to traditional education.

I will work toward the best library service
and access for all learners.

82

The Problem Patron

A soft answer turneth away wrath.

—Proverbs 15:1

In my experience, most people who use libraries are decent folk. The vast majority, not unexpectedly, take the library for granted and accept what they receive as a matter of course. Some few are in the habit of expressing gratitude with a thank you, a letter of commendation, or even a gift. Even fewer library users fall into the dread category of "problem patron." All of us have seen them arguing about fines, bullying student assistants or junior staff, throwing temper tantrums when they cannot immediately have exactly what they want, taking out the innumerable unknown frustrations of their lives on some poor staff member who can only guess at the source of their rage. We have all seen them marching off to complain to administrators and, occasionally, getting their way even when in the wrong. (Now, *there's* a way to boost staff morale.) We are supposed to smile, be accommodating, deflect the anger, and reserve our harsh words for the home or staff room. I think that we are often asked for more than we should give. Of course, we should rise above the situation, but none of us has "doormat" in our job description. It is a tricky job to balance dignity and service in the face of hostility and a refusal to accept that we are human too.

I will exhibit grace under pressure when dealing with problem patrons.

My Ideal Library

 I suppose all librarians, and many serious library users, have an ideal library somewhere in their minds. Mine is made up of aspects of many libraries and, alas, does not exist in one place. It is a small library in a small community somewhere in a region with a temperate climate. It was built more than fifty years ago of red brick and stone and combines the solidity and dignity of older libraries and the cheerfulness and light of the modern. It is a warm, quiet place; never empty and never crowded. The walls are alive with art . . . the plants healthy and well tended. There are books of all kinds, old and new, newspapers and journals, videos, sound recordings, and every other medium to use in the library or to borrow. The numerous computer terminals, sited in attractive, functional workstations, enable me to find any and all electronic resources. The staff are invariably interested and interesting, welcoming and helpful. It is always afternoon in my ideal library and shafts of sunlight fall on us—quiet library users in comfortable chairs, savoring the richness of learning and pleasure that the library offers.

I will see the ideal in every library.

Six

Present
& Future

Libraries and Democracy

Libraries are one of the only face-to-face services left where kids can come with no appointment and get professional services from someone with a master's degree who assigns no grades, makes no judgements. It's the greatest democratic institution ever created.

—Patrick O'Brien, quoted in "Outlook:
Will Libraries Survive?" *CQ Researcher*

Freely available, uncensored libraries are not only essential to democracy but also are inherently democratic. In making recorded knowledge and information available to all and in giving assistance in locating and using that recorded knowledge and information to all, we not only support democracy—we *are* democracy. An "elitist librarian," though there are some such, should be a contradiction in terms. Good library service weighs the needs and wants of library users and is indifferent to status, gender, race, age, religion, or any characteristics that too often divide us.

I will accept my role in supporting democracy.

E-mail in Libraries

Across the wires the electric message came.

—Alfred Austin, *Lines on the Illness*
of the Prince of Wales

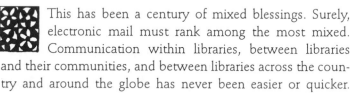 This has been a century of mixed blessings. Surely, electronic mail must rank among the most mixed. Communication within libraries, between libraries and their communities, and between libraries across the country and around the globe has never been easier or quicker. Meanwhile, never has so much time been wasted on one activity by so many. These are the two sides of the e-mail coin. It has given rise to innumerable invisible colleges of librarians discussing acquisitions, library education, circulation, reference, cataloguing, maps, music, and everything under the library sun. What a boon to enquiring minds that is—a species of electronic ALA conference going on twenty-four hours a day every day—but the participants are also discussing cats and recipes, sending flames and pointless anecdotes, gossiping, and generally shooting the breeze. The resemblance to an ALA conference is uncanny. Some administrators fear that e-mail's seductive power may divert effort from primary tasks. That is almost certainly so, but the e-mail genie is out of the bottle and likely to remain so—at least until the Internet is metered and as tamed as the telephone system.

I will use e-mail but not be obsessed by it.

The Tax Revolt

Politics is the art of the possible.

—R. A. Butler, *The Art of the Possible*

 I worry about librarians who say they "hate politics." All of us, from big city public librarians to rare book specialists in research libraries to grade school librarians to librarians in a national library, swim in a political sea. If we hate the element in which we swim or try to ignore it, we will drown or be washed up and stranded on some inconsequential shore. Money is the mother's milk of politics, as Jesse Unruh said, and the competition for "resources," to use the current euphemism, is one in which we must take part.

Librarians have been reasonably successful in social politics; our stands on intellectual freedom, gender equality, the rights of all minorities, literacy, etc., are well known, understood, and articulated. We are less effective when it comes to money politics. Witness the "Tax Revolt" in California in the 1970s—an eruption of greed that has crippled public policy and gutted public services in the Golden State. At the time, librarians were much exercised about the Equal Rights Amendment (ERA)—quite rightly—but paid little heed to the Tax Revolt, something that has a continuing malign effect on many libraries. For all that, we can and should "do" social politics and financial politics.

> *I will plunge into politics that affect the welfare of libraries and play an effective part in them.*

89

Copyright and Electronic Documents

Take away from English authors their copy-rights, and you will very soon take away from England her authors.

—Anthony Trollope, *Autobiography*

 Men and women create for a variety of reasons. These include the desire to communicate ideas and beliefs, to entertain, and to make art. They also include the desire to be famous, the wish to achieve tenure, and the sheer joy of seeing a name on a title page. These are all quite common motives and usually more than one is involved. However, the most common and pervasive motive is . . . money. A writer or artist is as worthy of recompense as anyone working in less exalted fields. Western societies have evolved a legal and practical structure over the last 100 years or so that ensures proper payment to the creator and owner of intellectual property. The structure consists of the publishing, production, and distribution industries and the copyright laws that are in force in almost all developed countries.

There are many fierce battles over copyright, to be sure, but they have been at the margins (what are the rights of a "ghost" writer? who owns the rights of a dead creator when the will is disputed? how many photocopies constitute "fair use"?). The central questions of intellectual property seemed essentially resolved and most writers and creators rewarded equitably. Until, that is, the advent of electronic documents and the promise of chaos ahead. I believe we will never solve

electronic copyright issues because the technology will always outrun the law, and the immensity of the Net will overshadow the moral concept of intellectual property.

> *I will help to ensure that writers and creators are rewarded and to safeguard affordable access for all.*

The Paper-Full Society

*If all the earth were paper white/And all the
sea were ink.*

—John Lyly, *Early Autobiographical Poems*

 One of the oddest ideas of recent decades is the
notion that we are moving into a "paperless society."
The Information Age was to be one of electronic
banking, electronic communication, paperless offices, electronic texts—a silent clean humming world with no need for
paper. The truth is that we are drowning in paper; paper that
is used for bank statements, bills, magazines, money, birthday
cards, and so on. Most offices keep paper copies of all correspondence, memoranda, forms, and even e-mail messages. As
they add more and more technology, libraries are finding that
the demand for printers attached to terminals, sophisticated
photocopiers, and even microform reader-printers continues
to increase exponentially. Library users want photocopies and
printouts of all kinds in ever increasing numbers and are willing to pay for them. There seems to be an almost atavistic
human need for the security and relative durability of print on
paper that is, so far, immune to the pundits of paperlessness.

I will encourage wise use of paper.

Downsizing

*It's a recession when your neighbor
loss his job.*

*It's a depression when you
lose your own.*

—Harry S. Truman, quoted
in the *Observer* (London)

 I am working on a law of librarianship that states, roughly, that when you hear a term that is (a) imported from management theory and (b) appears to have been translated literally from the German, you should watch out because someone is after your job. "Downsizing" and the even more repellent "rightsizing" are perfect examples. In all but a handful of cases, the large reductions in staff size they represent cannot be justified economically and have to be concealed in mumbo-jumbo masking antisocial priorities. There is an ethic of the bottom line in the private sector—one that states that some human beings are less important than profit. In the not-for-profit sector, in which most libraries reside, management gurus replace that for-profit ethic with appeals to efficiency. They call for being more "business-like" and for using automation to replace human beings. Balderdash! Libraries are already very cost-efficient because they have raised efficiency through technology and not increased costs. All libraries do far more with less, as compared to twenty-five years ago, than almost any other enterprise—public or private. Is it any wonder that librarians become demoralized when

these achievements, tremendous increases in service, and flexibility in adapting to change are rewarded with the brutality of downsizing? Perhaps we should be more aggressive in publicizing our many accomplishments and proclaiming our values in the face of soulless materialism.

> *I will upsize my self-esteem and that of my colleagues and take pride in our efficiency.*

Different in Kind

Civilization advances by extending the number of important operations that we can perform without thinking of them.

—Alfred North Whitehead, quoted in
Alan L. MacKay's *The Harvest of a Quiet Eye*

 Think of four everyday actions—reading a book or journal; logging on to the Internet; listening to a radio program; dialing a telephone number. Most of us do not think about such actions and how they differ—they are just part of modern communication. In the first two cases, you read or view a communication; in the other two, you listen or talk and listen. There is another, more important way of classifying them, however. When you read a book or listen to a radio, you are using the end product of communication without interacting with the machines that make it possible. Theoretically, it would be possible for every single person in the world to read the same book or listen to the same program simultaneously. On the other hand, if even a substantial minority of humankind were to log on to the Internet or dial a telephone number simultaneously, the systems would collapse. The capacity of the machines that make telephonic and Internet communication possible is crucial to their use and is intrinsically limiting, which is why the Internet and the Web are already creaking under the weight of use by what is still a relatively small minority of the world's population.

I will enjoy the benefits of technology but not be enslaved by it.

95

Virtual Lives

*With my library card I am rich. It is my access
to the inviting learning world.*

—Loreta Jordan (Washington, D.C.), quoted in the
ALA national campaign *Libraries Change Lives*

 We learn in three ways. First, by experiencing life. Second, by being taught by someone more knowledgeable and experienced than we are. Third, by reading books and interacting with other manifestations of recorded knowledge. Living, studying under a teacher, reading—these are the ingredients of learning that enable us to become knowledgeable, achieve understanding, and be wise. Life, classrooms, and libraries have been the environments of human development for centuries. Now, in the late twentieth century, some propose that human experience itself, already cheapened by the pervasiveness of television, may move into perpetual virtual reality; that the classroom is obsolete because of "distance learning" and "self-learning"; and that real libraries will be replaced by virtual libraries. Distance learning is not just a matter of replacing the classroom with interactive TV and cyberspace. It also posits changing the role of a teacher to that of a guide to self-learners freed from the authority of the learned. What is it about these times that breeds these virtual delusions and devaluations? Why are we expected to prefer the ersatz to the real? Start the virtual revolution without me, please.

I will value the reality that makes us real.

People or Kiosks?

One machine can do the work of fifty men.
No machine can do the work of one
*   extraordinary man.*

—Elbert Hubbard, quoted in
Roycroft's Dictionary and Book of Epigrams

 I have heard of academic libraries that have "reorganized" their reference departments to the point at which the primary interaction between students and library resources and programs takes place in a "kiosk." The latter is, essentially, a computer terminal with programs that guide the user through the undergrowth to the desired documents, texts, or images. Oh really? The librarians that survive such a reorganization are available for in-depth consultation with faculty and graduate students but the undergraduates have only the kiosk as guide, mentor, and friend.

When I contemplate this Timid New World scenario, I am amazed by the touching faith some library administrators have in machines and in the potential for artificial intelligence in dealing with real reference needs. Also, those administrators have not been looking at what is happening all around us. Banks are replacing mechanical services with human tellers. Telephone answering systems that pose an interminable series of multiple-choice questions are the object of universal ridicule and detestation. Human service is increasingly seen as the key to business success. People like to deal with people and libraries have been esteemed over the years because they provide human service.

I will not compromise the human dimension
of library service.

97

Museums of Failed Technology?

*The machines that are first invented
to perform any particular movement
are always the most complex.*

—Adam Smith, *Essay on the Principles
Which Lead and Direct Philosophical Inquiries*

 Every librarian has been burdened by one or more stereotypes. The oddest, to me, is the "librarian-as-Luddite," an image popular among techies and administrators. The truth is that we have been, if anything, *over*eager in our embrace of technology. Think about those 8-track tapes, U-Matic systems that eat their offspring, punched card systems, ingenious shelving arrangements orphaned by long bankrupt companies, expensive early computers with no replacement parts, and on and on. On the positive side, we have dared to try and fail occasionally, and at the end of it the library is often the most automated part of a campus, company, school, or community and the librarians are seen as pioneers by the people they serve. So, is it to be Luddite or technocrat? As ever, the answer lies in judgment and the use of whichever means promise best to accomplish the task.

*I will embrace library technology,
but not blindly.*

Library or Pipeline?

As often as a study is cultivated by little minds, they will draw from it narrow conclusions.

—John Stuart Mill, *Auguste Comte and Positivism*

 Some brainstorming by telecommunications experts, library administrators, and computer specialists has spawned the notion of future library service as a kind of pipeline to homes and offices with the library itself recast in the image of a utility. The "library utility" would deliver "information" to individuals via this pipeline, much as other utilities deliver electricity, natural gas, telephone service, and water. Leaving aside that such an idea ignores recorded knowledge and even downgrades "information" to the level of electricity or water (materials that can be used without need of interpretation by human minds), one is still struck by the extraordinary littleness of this idea, the narrowness of vision, and paucity of human understanding and imagination. Moreover, the "library utility" represents the ultimate, thus far, in the commodification and potential commercialization of library service. Instead of the rich, humane interplay of collections in all formats, library services, library staff, and library users, we have a mean matter of pipelines, switches, cables, fees, and inequality of access. Surely some ardent technocrat somewhere can do better than that.

I will cultivate a higher vision of libraries and their future.

Night Thoughts

To waste long nights in pensive discontent.

—Edmund Spenser, *Complaints,*
Mother Hubbard's Tale

 Sometimes, late in the evening or at night, I wonder what the world would be like if all the information futurists and advocates of technology *über alles* are actually right. Because the track record of technological prophecy is, to be polite, dismal, betting against such prophets is safe ninety-nine times out of a hundred. After all, not many of us read microfiche newspapers while taking our personal helicopter to work happily leaving diligent robots to clean our plastic houses. Technology generally confounds our expectations and its consequences, good and bad, are rarely foreseen. Perhaps, then, it is foolish to worry that this might be the one time in a hundred and haunt the watches of the night with the specters of the death of the book, the end of reading, the creation of a huge aliterate underclass, the reduction of higher education to television and the penciling of "Scantron" cards, and all the other joyless, gray outcomes of the vision of the wired intelligentsia. Anyway, day always comes and the nightmares recede. It is difficult to be pessimistic in the sunlight when both life and libraries look good.

I will be optimistic and remember time
heals all futurist fantasies.

Seven

Librarians

The Image of the Librarian

I was the pride of the public library . . .
until I discovered Smirnoff.

—1965 advertising slogan

 Librarians worry about their image more than those in most other professions. We have good reason to suppose that the general public, conditioned by the idea of Marian the Librarian, believes that we are all retiring if not antisocial; myopic due to years of promiscuous reading; repressed and rule obsessed; and fanatical about maintaining the silence of the tomb in our libraries. Beyond this characterization are the ignorance about and derogation of what we do. "It must be nice working in a library—all that time to read books." "Why do you need a master's degree to stamp books?" Few of us have not heard variations on these remarks many times over. Personally, I am not as bothered by Raymond Chandler's stereotype of "acid faced virgins . . . who stamp books" (*The High Window,* 1943) as by our reaction to it. Why do we masochistically collect even mildly derogatory remarks and, worse, write about them? Worst of all, why do we turn our backs on our own profession and take refuge in electronic fantasies in which Marian is transformed into an alluring "knowledge navigator" or "cybrarian"? We should turn from these responses and take a healthy pride in what we do and a large dose of pity for those who stereotype any group—including librarians.

I will take pride in the fact that librarians are
as diverse as the populations they serve.

103

Learning to Be a Librarian

*Experience, the universal mother
of the sciences.*

—Miguel de Cervantes, *Don Quixote*

 Though cynics say experience is a bald man's comb, I think it an essential part of learning to be a librarian. To some, education is the indispensable element of good librarianship, to others, experience in a library. The former expect library schools to turn out fully fledged librarians, the latter regard attendance at a library school as something that must be endured. Both are a little right and mostly wrong. Library schools are about educating librarians in all aspects of our profession: opening their eyes to the possibilities and practicalities of librarianship. Subsequent work in a library should be as important a part of the learning experience, something that adds value to library school education and transforms us into autonomous professionals. It is easy to criticize library schools as being too removed from the actualities of library life. We should also criticize those practicing librarians who expect too much from new colleagues, put nothing into training or mentoring, and do not work to provide positive experience.

*I will play my part in helping new colleagues
to learn to be librarians.*

Mysteries

I love to lose myself in a mystery . . .

—Sir Thomas Browne, *Religio Medici*

 I firmly believe, though I have neither research nor statistics to back me up, that the favorite book genre for librarians is the mystery novel. (I have also noticed, over the years, that many of us are assiduous crossword puzzle solvers.) There is, of course, something intellectually high-toned about mysteries that is completely lacking in Westerns, romance novels, and the rest. Thus it is that a librarian who would push a Danielle Steel novel under the sofa when visitors come will happily leave an Elmore Leonard or Martha Grimes out for everyone to see. I think there are deeper reasons, though. Librarians are trained by education and experience to love order and to find things out. It is easy to see the allure of a mystery novel when it is compared to the imperfect world of the reference desk—with its sometimes unanswerable questions—or the cataloguing department—with its materials that sometimes refuse to fit into the lovely logic of the Rules. All issues are resolved and logic prevails in good mystery stories, and what is the supersleuth anyway but a sort of transcendental librarian who answers everybody's questions? Detectives in modern mysteries are often unappreciated toilers in less than glamorous vineyards—small wonder we librarians find them sympathetic!

I will enjoy the mysteries and puzzles of library work.

The Impossibility of Classification

Knowledge is multi-dimensional and the
number of dimensions tends to the infinite.

—S. R. Ranganathan

Every day, in libraries throughout the world, cataloguers perform a feat of dazzling intellectual audacity. They classify books and other materials. In other words, they reduce the infinite dimensions of knowledge to a straight line from 000 to 999 or A to Z. There is an old cartoon of a gamekeeper and a fisherman. The first says "You can't fish here" to which the fisherman replies "I *am* fishing here." Classification, the thing that cannot be done, is done all the time by librarians. The amazing thing is that it works—classification numbers, those dots on the straight line, enable library users to locate materials and groups of materials with great ease and are used more and more in online systems to provide sophisticated subject access. All this because librarians do something impossible without turning a hair!

I will value the work of cataloguers and
use the tools they provide.

Political Correctness?

The right words in the right order.

—Aleksander Blok's definition of poetry

 Librarian Sandy Berman is chiefly famous for his trumpet blast against the Library of Congress *List of Subject Headings* (*Prejudices and Antipathies,* 1971). He helped to prompt the Library of Congress to update its vocabulary and to remove terms that are offensive to groups and classes of persons. There is a basic tension, however, between two tenets of the Berman approach: that vocabulary should reflect what is in common use today (known in the trade as the "sought heading") on the one hand, and the laudable imperative to remove prejudice from the vocabulary on the other. For many people in this country, the sought heading for certain groups of the far North would be "Eskimo"—a term that has offensive connotations to the groups themselves. They use and want others to use "Inuit." This topic ties in with the empty term "politically correct," used to stigmatize those who try to be sensitive in their choice of words and prefer descriptive neutral terms for groups and other social phenomena.

So what is it to be—in subject headings and in social discourse—the term most in use or the correct, descriptive term? I believe in the educational power of words and, in close cases, would lean to the side of nonprejudicial, neutral terms in the hope they would prevail. It is not so long, after all, since Native Americans were routinely referred to as "Indians" and their nations as "tribes." We know better now on this and many other topics, in part because we have sought to civilize our subject headings.

I will not be discouraged in my use of bias-free language.

107

ALA Conferences

*My life's been a meeting, Dad, one long
meeting. Even on the few committees I
don't yet belong to, the agenda winks at
me as I pass.*

—Gwyn Thomas, *The Keep*

 American Library Association conferences have become, as Henry James said of Victorian novels, "great
loose, baggy monsters"—librarians and exhibitors by
the thousands gathering in cold cities in the winter and swel-
tering cities in the summer. A great throng of humanity in a
never-ending round of programs, meetings, breakfasts, lunches,
dinners, and informal colloquies in bars, lobbies, elevators,
sidewalks, and stairwells. All these people milling around in
sensible shoes in search of enlightenment and the furtherance
of our profession.

I have been to many "ALAs," have spoken, served on
committees, listened, visited the exhibits, and partaken of the
social life. Is it worth it? What, as the little boy said, is the con-
ference *for*? It would be easy to be cynical and stress the
undoubted *longueurs* and the massed egos on parade. It would
also be wrong, because ALA conferences are about two very
important things—learning and companionship. It is probably
true that attendees learn more in informal ways than they do
from programs, but they do learn. The companionship matters
because we need to know that we share and are willing to
work together for goals, ideals, and values in a world that is
often inimical to all three.

*I will look beyond the meetings
for the meanings.*

108

Problem Colleagues

Them which is of other naturs thinks different.

—Mrs. Gamp in Charles Dickens'
Martin Chuzzlewit

 Most of the hundreds of people with whom I have worked over the decades have been wise, kind, agreeable, pleasant in thought, word, and deed, or, at least, tolerable. Hardly surprising, because libraries attract people who are by and large cultured, civilized, and collegial. However, there are the few exceptions and I, like most of us, have had to work for and with the sullen, egotistical, domineering, and only marginally sane. There are people who seem neither to invite nor wish for pleasant working relationships. There are supervisors who belittle when they should praise, derogate when they should encourage. There are peers who bring competition into the cooperative ambience of libraries. There are subordinates who see advice as an affront and cannot accept guidance. I cherish the memory of the many harmless and interesting eccentrics with whom I have worked but think far less fondly of the mean, malign, and the scheming. I know it behooves us to remember that obnoxious behavior often arises from insecurity and fear, but it is difficult to rise above natural human reactions. In the long run, the best thing to do is to strive for as much accommodation as is compatible with human dignity.

I will endeavor to get on with annoying colleagues and to ignore the intolerable.

109

The Library "Great Person"

*Genius is the talent for seeing things straight.
It is seeing things in a straight line without any
bend or break or aberration of sight, seeing
them as they are, without any warping of
vision. Flawless mental sight! That's genius.*

—Maude Adams, quoted in
Maude Adams: A Biography

 I have been privileged to meet, and in some cases to
know, some of the people who have had a profound
effect on modern librarianship. It is hard to look into
the history of libraries without coming away with the idea that
Carlyle was right and it is individuals not blind forces that
shape history. It is in the story of those people and the impact
that they had, the causes they championed, and the legacy
they left, that we can understand how great libraries are
formed, innovations in library service are made, and our profession and its world changed forever. Maude Adams' definition of genius makes me think of, among others, Jesse Shera,
S. R. Ranganathan, Fred Kilgour, Eva Verona, Seymour
Lubetzky, Augusta Baker, Hugh Atkinson, and A. J. Wells. A
clear vision and a sense of purpose informed their professional
lives as it did those of Melvil Dewey, Margaret Mann,
Anthony Panizzi, and the many other library "great persons"
that I know only from their writings and deeds. Let us hope
that our profession will continue to be enriched by many such
people, now and in the future.

*I will celebrate great librarians and draw
inspiration from their accomplishments.*

110

The Outsider Syndrome

Let the cobbler stick to his last.

—Pliny the Elder, *Natural History*

Librarians of Congress are not, with the notable exception of Quincy Mumford, librarians. They have come from various walks of life ranging from literary figures (such as Archibald MacLeish) to dodgy academics. Whatever their qualities and defects, the fact remains that they have been charged with running an enterprise that has practices, methods, principles, and an internal culture to which they are strangers. Some major academic libraries also have been headed by nonlibrarians. This is almost invariably the case in Asia and some European countries; the fact that these libraries are greatly inferior in services to American academic libraries is no coincidence.

There is something deep in the American psyche that distrusts certain expertise. Why else is the term "professional politician" one of opprobrium and whence otherwise the enthusiasm for businesspeople and soldiers as potential presidents? Today, generals run school districts but no teachers command armies; accountants run hospitals but no physicians head stockbroking firms; and academics run libraries but no librarians head, say, history departments. I have known personally three librarians who would have made great Librarians of Congress but were never considered. Odd, is it not, that a lifetime of experience and expertise counts for nothing at the top.

I will value and defend my expertise and that of all trained librarians.

111

The War of AACR2

Jaw-jaw is better than war-war.

—Harold Macmillan, paraphrasing
Winston Churchill

 The War of AACR2 was waged bitterly in the later 1970s. It concerned the impact and the extent of the descriptive cataloguing changes to be caused by the introduction of the second edition of the *Anglo-American Cataloguing Rules*. Like all small wars it mattered everything to the participants and nothing to the rest of the world. It was about important things even though it reminded outsiders of the battle of the Big-endians and the Little-endians in *Gulliver's Travels* (concerning the right end to open a boiled egg). The questions were: how much was a truly modern cataloguing code worth? how were the records of the past to be updated? can catalogues be changed incrementally? At the heart of all the heat and less light was a failure of communication between cataloguers and library administrators—the latter feeling, with little justification, they had been ambushed by the former. It ended as all wars do, in face-saving and inefficient compromise. It was so long ago and, now that AACR2 is so entrenched, so pointless-seeming and so avoidable.

I will take the long view when faced with change.

Women in Libraries

*. . . Libraries represent a rare example of
a civic environment dominated by women.*

—Thomas Hine, reviewing a book
on Carnegie libraries in the
New York Times Book Review

 Beginning about 100 years ago, prompted by Andrew Carnegie's philosophy, it was mainly women who did the work of creating a vast public library system. To this day, eight of ten librarians—and a higher percentage of other library workers—are women. On the other hand, women are still proportionately underrepresented at the top levels of library management, especially in academic libraries, though the ratios are improving. Any objective observer of librarianship will conclude that our profession has been shaped by women and has a very different ethos from historically male professions. Service, cooperation, and selfless dedication to the common good are central to our working lives. These are things to celebrate, things that make me glad to be a librarian and a feminist. Perhaps the "feminist" here is tautologous—how could a librarian not be dedicated to the advancement of equal opportunity for women in all spheres of life?

*I will support the advancement of women
and celebrate what women achieve.*

113

A Word for Ned Ludd

A little rebellion now and then is a good thing.

—Thomas Jefferson, letter to James Madison

 Ned Ludd may or may not have existed. The Luddite "movement" with which he is identified was a sporadic series of acts by desperately poor workers who feared the change presaged by new technology. They were savagely repressed, and those who lived saw the triumph of machines. To this day, anyone raising concerns about the introduction of technology and consequent societal displacement is called a "Luddite." In truth, those long-ago workers were fighting to preserve a way of life as well as their jobs. The result of the technology they opposed—the Industrial Revolution—created misery for millions over many generations. To label as Luddites those who argue caution about the "computer revolution" and its consequent "downsizing" is convenient but intellectually dishonest.

Up to now, computer technology in libraries has been almost entirely beneficial. It has enhanced service, made us more cost-efficient, and provided many useful sources of information. What is to be feared is not the advances we have made but the encroachment of technology into areas in which it does not belong; the loss of a culture based on the sustained reading of texts; and the debasing of society. Is that irrational?

I will welcome useful technological innovation and keep it in its place.

Eight

Places

The Library as a Public Place

A place for everything, and everything in its place.

—Samuel Smiles, *Thrift*

 Librarians are often forced into a utilitarian view of library buildings. That is why many modern libraries may work very well but fail to lift the spirit. The last few decades have seen too many libraries that exalt function over form. Look at even the smallest nineteenth-century libraries and see how the communities and colleges that built them knew that a library is more than a place that works well. A library is, and should be, a public place; a center of the life of its community. And that library should embody the aspirations of the members of that community—not only through its collections and services but also as a place that houses communal activities and the exhibits that feed the community's hunger for art and enlightenment. That is why a library building should never be, to adapt the French architect Le Corbusier, simply a machine for storing and delivering recorded knowledge and information, but rather a fit embodiment of the higher ideals of humankind.

I will understand the importance of the library as a public place.

117

National Libraries

When a don asked me how many books I had,
I really couldn't reply but this didn't matter. I
was too polite to deliver a variant of Samuel
Butler's "I keep my books round the corner, in
the British Museum."

—Philip Larkin, quoted in *Books for All*

 Although all libraries do what my late friend Hugh Atkinson called "the Lord's work," there is something magnificent about the very idea of a national library. Although they came about in very different ways, each of the world's national libraries has a simply stated but breathtaking mission—to collect and make available all books and other materials published in that nation or pertaining to that nation. Whether planned (like France's Bibliothèque Nationale) or verging on the accidental (Thomas Jefferson's library became the core of the Library of Congress, today the greatest national library of them all), national libraries aspire to be their nation's memory, heart, and mind. In many cases, they chase the unattainable dream of being a universal library.

In this time when nationalism—both a curse and a high cultural impulse—and established states do not always coincide, one could almost define a nation as an entity possessing a national library. Beyond the narrowness of nationalistic concerns, though, we can find inspiration in the internationalism of, and cooperation between, the great national libraries of the world.

I will take pride in national libraries, even
as we seek to transcend nationalism.

Cotleigh Road Branch Library

We shape our buildings, thereafter they shape us.

—Winston Churchill, quoted in *Time*

 It was a turn-of-the-century library set in a row of terraced houses on a slight hill in a poor area of North London. A lot of the people who used it and, in many cases, spent long hours there were Irish immigrants and refugees from central Europe. To a young man in thrall to the magic of libraries, it was an entire world that taught lessons of service to all—to the retirees who rushed to commandeer favored newspapers on rainy mornings; to the romance novel–reading woman with three small children; to the children engrossed by a puppet show. It was a small library in an ill-favored area but it mattered to the people who lived there as great and small libraries matter to communities today.

I will remember the importance of libraries to every user.

Beyond the Museum

The time was *when a library was very like a museum and the librarian a mouser in musty books. The time* is *when the library is a school and the librarian in the highest sense a teacher . . .*

—Melvil Dewey, quoted in *Books for All*

The highest calling in civilized societies is that of teacher. More than entertainers, politicians, and lawyers, and as much as doctors, the teacher stands for civilization, for the shared wisdom of the ages, for the improvement of society, and for disinterested goodness. Even in today's material world, the idea of someone sharing and inducing knowledge and understanding is powerful. What is a saint, a priest, a guru, a sage, a shaman but a teacher of the higher kind?

Melvil Dewey, in saying that librarianship had moved so far beyond museum-like curating that librarians had become teachers, was making a most important claim. Libraries *are* schools in the broadest sense, and librarians *do* teach, directly and indirectly. We are opening the door to knowledge just in organizing our materials so that they can be readily located. In reference work and library instruction, we are not just imparting facts but making it possible for learning and understanding to take place. As any good teacher will tell you, creating a climate of learning is the best achievement; showing the path and clearing the way to knowledge the highest goal.

I will think of myself as a teacher and will teach.

120

Ssshh!

*The meditative mind flows in this silence and
love is the way of this mind.*

—J. Krishnamurti,
The Second Penguin Krishnamurti Reader

 A national magazine article ("Silence, Please," *Harper's,*
1997) decries the transformation, as the writer sees it,
of the library from a place of contemplative quiet to a
noisy realm of "information access." Libraries have a long and
noble role as a universal haven for those who seek a quiet
place to read, think, and write. The author, Sallie Tisdale,
makes a reasonable point in suggesting that this role may have
been fatally compromised by our desire to rid ourselves of our
image as shushing nags and to become all things to all users. I
think it wrong, though, to blame the terminals and electronic
media for this change. Nor do I think that the peace of the past
is incompatible with the flash and glitz of the present. It is per-
fectly possible to have quiet areas and what amount to computer arcades in the same building, but surely it is societal
norms that have changed and not the essential nature of the
library. Noise blares everywhere today. Loud unwatched TVs
and music that must be popular with some invade all our public spaces. We can provide library places in which people can
hear themselves think . . . but do contemporary users want
them? Let us hope so, and hope that there will always be a
demand for silence and thought.

I will provide quiet places in the library.

Prisons

All we know who lie in gaol
Is that the wall is strong;
And that each day is like a year
A year whose days are long.

—Oscar Wilde,
The Ballad of Reading Gaol

 It has been said that the only good things that ever came from prisons are the books written there. There is a rich vein of literature, from John Bunyan to Vaclav Havel, written in and about prisons. However, very few prisoners produce literary works and, for the vast majority, books are not their creation but their recreation. This has been a dreadful century in so many ways and the number of the imprisoned has been greater in our time than any other. Reading offers both mental freedom and an avenue to a better future. Therefore, in supplying books and other library services, prison librarians are doing a great service to the imprisoned and to the society that will benefit from any rehabilitation. The state of California, for the first time in history, spent more on prisons than it did on education in 1995/1996. The same dismal trend is seen elsewhere. Clearly, society must consider the consequences of mass imprisonment and remedies for its effects very carefully. Prison librarians are manifestations of the better angels of our nature in the penal system and we all owe them a debt.

I will remember my prison library colleagues
in their struggle to change lives.

122

Home Base

When we build, let us think that we build for ever.

—John Ruskin, *The Seven Lamps of Architecture*

 When the eighty-four-year-old county central library in Portland, Oregon, showed signs of age and decrepitude, the citizens of Multnomah County passed a thirty-million-dollar bond guaranteeing the renovation, wiring, and seismic bracing of the library. Bucking the national trend toward tearing down old library buildings and replacing them with glass and steel structures, "Central" in Portland has been updated, made safer, and restored to its state in a time when civic buildings made grand statements about community. This is probably not surprising in the capital of Ecotopia—a city and a county in which seventy in a hundred citizens have library cards; a place of bookishness and environmental concern going hand in hand with respect for tradition and old buildings. In a gesture of physical as well as financial support, more than 1,000 volunteers helped in the move of the library's books from temporary accommodation. One volunteer, a five-decade user of Central, put it best when he said, "This was the center of my intellectual world. This is home base."

I will help to preserve and extend the use of useful library buildings.

Libraries and the Mall

Because, you see, the main thing today is—
shopping. Years ago a person, he was unhappy,
didn't know what to do with himself—he'd go
to church . . . Today, you're unhappy? . . .
Go shopping!

—Arthur Miller, *The Price*

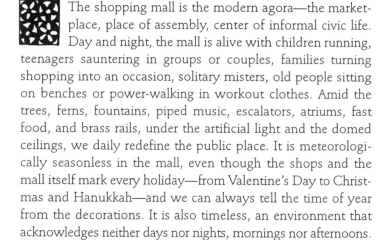 The shopping mall is the modern agora—the market-
place, place of assembly, center of informal civic life.
Day and night, the mall is alive with children running,
teenagers sauntering in groups or couples, families turning
shopping into an occasion, solitary misters, old people sitting
on benches or power-walking in workout clothes. Amid the
trees, ferns, fountains, piped music, escalators, atriums, fast
food, and brass rails, under the artificial light and the domed
ceilings, we daily redefine the public place. It is meteorologi-
cally seasonless in the mall, even though the shops and the
mall itself mark every holiday—from Valentine's Day to Christ-
mas and Hanukkah—and we can always tell the time of year
from the decorations. It is also timeless, an environment that
acknowledges neither days nor nights, mornings nor afternoons.

With all its faults it is our place, it is what we have.
Nostalgia cannot re-create the town square and the old downtown in their original form and we must live in today not in
memory. A German woman once said to me, "I hate these
malls. Forty places to buy shoes and nowhere to buy an
apple!" However that may be, the mall is where the people are

124

and where you will find a concentration of all kinds of folk. That is why libraries belong in malls as much as shoe stores and as surely as they belonged in the old town square.

> *I will locate library services where members of my community like to be.*

California Dreams

> *If we cannot now end our differences, at least
> we can make the world safe for diversity.*
>
> —John F. Kennedy, speech at American University

 Oakland is over the Bay from San Francisco. It is famous as the home of Jack London and well known for Oaklander Gertrude Stein's description—"there's no there there when you get there." It is a diverse community used to struggling with adversity. If you ever doubt the ability of "big government" to do good or, specifically, the achievements of the now-supplanted federal Library Services and Construction Act (LSCA), consider the "Chinatown" area of Oakland and its Oakland P.L. Asian Branch Library. It is in a community of people of Asian heritage from many countries—China, Japan, Korea, Thailand, Burma, Cambodia, Laos, the Philippines, and Vietnam.

The Asian Library was founded with the assistance of an LSCA grant in 1975 and moved a number of times before settling in its present site. It contains materials in English and all the languages of the community and has a multilingual staff. Here is a wonderful example of a city reaching out to serve a distinct group and cherishing the diversity that is at the heart of the true American dream. Oakland is helping the whole community from older people in a strange land who may never learn English to adults and children who need materials and services in their own languages as they cross the bridge to the English proficiency that most want.

> *I will cherish and nurture cultural diversity
> in my community.*

Art and Decoration in the Library

The object of art is to give life a shape.

—Jean Anouilh, *The Rehearsal*

 As I write, you can find the following in my library: a large set of prints by the noted artist Henry Evans; an exhibition of black-and-white California nature photographs (school of Ansel Adams); numerous artificial but real-looking green plants; portraits of each of the university's former presidents; a number of ALA "Read" posters starring Cesar Chavez, Golda Meir, Marlee Matlin, and others (the Elvis was stolen); various paintings of local scenes; exhibits on the WWII Japanese internment and Hmong culture; a weekly display of maps of places in the news (e.g., Bosnia); and various bronzes (nudes from the collection of a local benefactor). All this is quite apart from the posters, photographs, statuettes, and African violets with which staff members decorate their work areas. Each library is an individual public place and each is adorned with things of beauty and local interest. Why is this? I believe the desire to beautify and individualize arises from the ancient, deep human need to make every place a "home" and to please and interest the "guests" in that home. We are linked inexorably to the cave dwellers of tens of thousands of years ago and to everyone in between.

I will beautify my library to honor its guests.

"The Flowering of the Imagination"

*In the reading room in the New York Public
Library
All sorts of souls were bent over in silence
reading the past,
Or the present, or maybe it was the future,
persons
Devoted to silence and the flowering of the
imagination . . .*

—Richard Eberhart, *Reading Room,
the New York Public Library*

 This is a wonderful image—the silent flowering of many imaginations in one of the great civic buildings of a world city. The silence of such a library is neither negative nor imposed; it is the silence of creativity, the self-imposed silence of those who are concentrating on absorbing knowledge and transmuting it in the crucible of a unique mind. All the "souls" that Eberhart saw were engaged in a mysterious, ever-different process. The magic of reading is in the voices of the past and present speaking to us and each of us hearing those voices in distinctly different ways.

We each have our own Shakespeare—an infinity of readers in an infinity of libraries would produce an infinity of interpretations of every poem, play, and line in the canon of that complex genius. In Shakespeare, as in the work of every great writer, we read of the past, present, and future and, when things go right, our imaginations flower and our lives

and views of our lives change. In the daily rounds of library work, amid all the prosaic details and repetitious tasks, we should always be conscious of the brilliant mental life that is flowering all around us.

> *I will remember that everything we do*
> *contributes to the development of minds.*

The Love of Libraries

We love the things we love for what they are.

—Robert Frost, *Hyla Brook*

 It is not fashionable today to admit a love for libraries but people have written poems to libraries and have written essays on their beauty in the past. Tyrants have sought to destroy libraries not only because of what they contain but also because hate-filled people hate what others love. The destruction of churches, libraries, and other public buildings in the former Yugoslavia arose from a recognition of the importance to a culture and society of buildings that transcend their everyday use. From the dawn of libraries to the present day, each age has redefined what constitutes beauty in building. However, the purpose of creating libraries remains that of building a place that works but is also conducive to learning (as ugly places cannot be) and uplifts the community, large or small, for which the library is built. I have memories of the sight, sound, and atmosphere of many libraries. Those memories contain a keen knowledge of what made each library important and attractive to library users and nonusers alike. We need libraries that we can love—buildings that are important to the citizens of a locality, state, or nation and to members of a university, college, or school. We need them because symbols of learning and civilization matter—they inspire the human spirit.

I will love library buildings for what they are and for what they symbolize.

130

Nine

Reading
& Writing

Electronic "Books"

I sing the book electric.

—With apologies to Walt Whitman,
I Sing the Body Electric

 The most immutable law of all is the Law of Unintended Consequences. For example, the interstate highway project of the 1950s was not intended to lead to the devastation of many small towns and the rise of chains of franchised motels. What was briefly called "the information superhighway" may well lead to equally unpleasant and pleasant surprises. If access to the I-Way is to depend less and less on texts and typing and more and more on images and clicking, what will be the effect on the ability of children to acquire the ability to read and pleasure in reading? At the other end of the spectrum we have the various projects (Project Gutenberg being the best known), dedicated to digitizing the texts of classics of world literature—almost all of which are, not coincidentally, out of copyright.

If the only tool you have is a hammer, everything looks like a nail. To those who can only see the computer as the answer to everything, it must make perfect sense to take *The Woman in White,* an old translation of Dante's *Inferno,* and *The Last of the Mohicans* and key or scan them (or, more accurately, one version of them) so that they can be retrieved from the Internet. Others might ask "What for?" Not only are all these works widely available in inexpensive, high-quality paperbacks (for them, too, copyright is not an issue) but they are also unusable on the screen and must be printed to be

read. My Penguin *Woman in White* runs to more than 500 pages. At four cents a page, that is twenty dollars plus for a vastly inferior unbound printout. Not much of a bargain. However, the unintended consequence is that electronic texts are invaluable for textual scholars. So, projects intended to benefit mass audiences end up being tools for a very small, intensely specialized group. And so it goes . . .

> *I will seek to use available tools*
> *most effectively.*

The Gift of Reading

The power of good literature can be a life force.

—Ken Gallegos, "Grandmother's Powerful
Gift of Literacy," *Fresno Bee,* 1996

 The politicians and the people complain that children can't (or, more likely, won't) read. Libraries are one answer and reading to children another. We can soothe and entertain the very young with simple stories and picture books. We can go on to introduce them to a private pleasure of infinitely more complexity and reward than the drivel that infests most of children's TV. We can help the children to discover the pleasure of words, the humor and the pathos of life, and its inexhaustible complexity and abundance. Through reading come other skills. No one who is ill-read can write well. Reading teaches us logic and the story of humankind, and an ever-expanding vocabulary is the fertile soil in which the seeds of knowledge flourish. What is wonderful is that it can all start with the simplest human interaction—a grandparent, parent, or friend reading to a small, probably sleepy child. In that quiet, humdrum connection we can see a true family value—the gift of a key to a door that will open on an infinity of marvels—and the human love between family and friends that nurtures the love of words, the love of books, and the lifelong journey of literacy and learning.

*I will read to children and show them
the wonders of reading.*

The Continuum of Literacy

*There is an art of reading as well as an art of
thinking and an art of writing.*

—Isaac D'Israeli, *Literary Character*

 Many worthy people devote much time to the question of literacy and take steps to overcome the evil of illiteracy. Controversy rages about the best way in which to teach children to read but all agree that, no matter the method, the goal is good. There are inspiring stories of people who have hidden their illiteracy well into adulthood and then had their lives enriched by the dedication of adult literacy teachers. These are noble efforts, and I look forward to the time when every child is literate and there is no such thing as adult illiteracy. On the other hand, I do believe that there is something limiting about the general literacy effort. That limitation arises from the dualistic assumption that one is either literate or illiterate; that there is a river to be crossed from the left bank of illiteracy to the right bank of reading. We do acknowledge a halfway state in which one is "functionally literate"—that is, has the minimal ability to read forms, tabloid newspapers, etc. Literacy is a much more complex matter than these formulations allow. Learning to read is but the first step in what should be a lifelong journey. No one is just literate—having learned to read we should become more and more literate as the years go by. There is an art to reading and we need to practice that art constantly if our minds are to develop fully.

*I will take nonreaders beyond
functional literacy.*

The Ladder of Learning

*It is a great nuisance that knowledge can only
be acquired by hard work.*

—W. Somerset Maugham, *Novels and Their Authors*

 Mortimer Adler, the founding father of the Great
Books movement, has delineated a most useful concept of the structure of learning. He identifies "four
goods of the mind" that illuminate the way in which human
beings understand and relate to the physical and mental
world. Unlike the process of physical aging—that bell curve
that goes from the helplessness of childhood through the
prime of life to the vicissitudes of age—the process of learning
can be always onward and upward. The human mind can go
from the blissful ignorance of the infant to the limitless possibilities of the developed mind.

Adler's "four goods" are, in ascending order of importance: information, knowledge, understanding, and wisdom.
Information can be defined as data (facts in textual, visual, or
numeric form) and simple, discrete factual descriptions. These
are the elements that, when assembled and interpreted in context, are the basis of *knowledge*—something that is new and
greater than the sum of its parts. Informed people know facts,
knowledgeable people have interpreted those facts and fitted
them into a body of knowledge that is the necessary precondi-
tion of *understanding,* which, in turn, must come before *wisdom.*

Libraries provide information in many ways but provide recorded knowledge in only one principal way—texts

137

printed on paper. The use of libraries can lead to many outcomes, from the solution of practical problems through access to usable information, to the attainment of wisdom after sustained reading that has led to knowledge and understanding.

> *I will provide collections and services*
> *that will give library users the opportunity*
> *to become wise.*

Back to Basics?

True ease in writing comes from art not chance.

—Alexander Pope, *An Essay in Criticism*

 A common complaint of employers and college professors is that high school graduates today lack necessary reading, writing, and mathematical skills. A local employer told me that she had no objection to training new employees in the special needs of her business, but did expect them to be able to read with comprehension, write clear English sentences without misspellings, and do routine computations. Employers and professors often blame modern educational theory and practice and call for a return to "basics"—the Three Rs. There may or may not be some truth to their theory and it certainly could not hurt if all children could read, write, and do sums competently long before they leave high school.

What seems indisputable to me is that reading (and the lack of it) is at the heart of this issue. People who do not read cannot express themselves clearly in speech or writing and lack the nimbleness of mind that assists computation. There is no substitute for reading—certainly not "visual literacy," "computer literacy," or any like fiddle-faddle. Reading programs should be seen for what they are—vital to our economic and cultural survival.

I will work with teachers and parents as they strive to give children the life skills they need.

Paperbacks

*The traveler who is lonely should always take
a book as his companion.*

—Oriental saying, quoted in
M. Ia Telepin's *Pokhlava Kniga*

 The mass-market paperback book was invented more than 100 years ago for the train traveler. The idea was that books intended to divert travelers need not be durable because they were to be read and then discarded. The station bookstall became common—its modern descendant can be seen in every airport today. A disposable artifact for the convenience of the traveler gave rise to one of the great economic, technological, and cultural marvels of the twentieth century.

Few recognize that marvel—the very omnipresence of paperbacks hides their economy, adaptability, and user-friendliness and the way they reach untold millions by catering to every taste and interest. Until comparatively recently, libraries regarded them as being somehow unworthy to be added to collections. We now collect them routinely because of advances in binding and paper quality and the advent of the "trade" paperback—much more durable than its mass-market cousin. What began as an amusement for the sooty Victorian train traveler is now a mass communications phenomenon and a respected part of library collections.

*I will value paperbacks and all the other
products of popular culture.*

Library Literature

> *. . . to make that recollection as durable as*
> *possible by putting it in writing.*
>
> —Benjamin Franklin, *Autobiography*

 A cynic once added "library literature" to a list of well-known oxymorons (Utah Jazz, military intelligence, etc.). There *are* a number of not very well written articles and books in the field of librarianship, but not any more than can be found in most fields. Though little in library literature scales the heights, we can take consolation in the fact that little of it plumbs the depths reached by, for example, much modern literary criticism and information science writing. I like a lot of the articles published in general and specialized library journals and invariably find something interesting and informative in each issue. I even look kindly upon the despised "how we did it good in my library" article. There is often something to be learned from such accounts and I am cheered by both the authors' enthusiasm for their achievements and their willingness to share. When it comes to books on libraries and librarianship, there is a minority that stand out because they are well written and engaging, but it is a decent minority and something for which to be grateful.

> *I will learn from the writings of my colleagues*
> *and share my own knowledge and opinions.*

Collecting Books

> *. . . mine own library with volumes that*
> *I prize above my dukedom.*
>
> —William Shakespeare, *The Tempest*

I have every symptom of bibliomania other than kleptomania. I have collected books since—when very young—I fell in love with a set of the complete works of Thackeray in fifteen small red volumes priced at fifteen shillings (then about three dollars) in a London bookstore. I also fell in love with the secondhand bookstores themselves, and cannot enter one today without making a purchase. Books *do* furnish a room, as one of Anthony Powell's characters says, but that is not why we bibliomaniacs collect them. To tell the truth, I am not sure that I can express why I would sooner part with almost any of my possessions than my books, or why I need all the novels, dictionaries, anthologies, biographies, mystery stories, histories, and so on. We know that we do not *need* personal books—least of all librarian book collectors—but there is something about the way they speak to us unopened and spring to life when opened. It is good to sit at home in peace surrounded by the books that mean so much to me, even if neither utilitarianism nor rationalism can tell me why.

> *I will prize books both for their content and for*
> *the memories and values they embody.*

Jabberwocky

'Twas brillig and the slithy toves
Did gyre and gimbel in the wabe.

—Lewis Carroll, *Jabberwocky*

 Lewis Carroll made nonsense a literary style and has amused and intrigued generations. There is a gray literature of reports on the future of libraries that matches Carroll nonsense for nonsense but, alas, without the fun. They are almost always not by librarians and contain the following ingredients—a language that combines the worst of management and academic jargon and catchphrases; "solutions" without any basis in economic reality or practicality; and a naive reliance on electronic technology as the answer to all that ails us. Stir in a generous dollop of assertions about the Information Age and, voila!, another report causing sages to nod, administrators to highlight and forward passages to their subordinates, and librarians to sigh and then turn back to reality. Here is a short extract from a recent example:

> The library of the future will be about access and knowledge management, not about ownership. The hurdles that will be faced in creating this new electronic environment will most likely come from our unwillingness to break from our competitive tendencies, our parochialism, and our unwillingness to accept the inevitability of change.

Note the neat rhetorical double whammy. The author implies that libraries are not currently about access and "knowledge

management" and that anyone who doubts the cockamamy solution proposed is a competitive, parochial mossback.

I will endure ill-informed speculations
with equanimity and cheerfulness.

The Library Hand

*And I copied all the letters in a big
round hand.*

—W. S. Gilbert, *H.M.S. Pinafore*

 Most who have used the huge card catalogues of
long-established research libraries will have come
across handwritten cards in a form of writing called
the Library Hand. You could almost believe that those old
cards were written by the same person since the Library Hand,
once acquired, was as predictable and readable on the nineti-
eth card of the day as it was on the first. Early library students
were taught the Hand in order to ensure that catalogue cards,
acquisition ledgers, and all the other written records of nine-
teenth- and early twentieth-century libraries were uniform and
uniformly readable. Some library schools then also taught
tachygraphy ("the art or practice of rapid writing"). One can
almost see those earnest starched students, presided over, if
legend is correct, by Melvil Dewey himself, tongue between
the teeth as they wielded steel nibs and blue/black ink in the
battle to achieve a balance between accuracy, readability, and
speed. Remember these were the days when the new word
"typewriter" referred to a person not a machine.

There is something quaint about all this but it has its
modern counterparts. Computer programming was taught in
library schools with enthusiasm ten to twenty years ago.
Today, I am told, up-to-date library schools spend a great deal
of time teaching the mechanics of constructing Web pages.

The Library Hand and the making of Web pages are useful skills at the periphery of librarianship. Useful but transitory since they are always replaced by more efficient alternatives that free librarians to get on with the serious business at the heart of their profession.

I will not devote my energy to ephemeral skills.

Reading

My early and invincible love of reading,
which I would not exchange for the
treasures of India.

—Edward Gibbon, *Autobiography*

 We live in a time in which reading and the ability to read are simultaneously of great public concern and dismissed as unimportant. Politicians, editorialists, and parents worry about "why Johnny can't read" (more likely "doesn't read") while proclaiming that books are dying and electronic communication is on the verge of hegemony. Computer companies compete to create the most "user-friendly" systems—meaning systems that get computer users to what they want with the maximum of images and clicking and the minimum of words and typing. So, we bemoan the illiteracy and aliteracy of our children, console ourselves with the lazy myth that they are all "computer literate," and ignore the fact that, at the end of the day when all the icons have gone and the clicking has ceased, those same children will be presented with . . . texts! The mind cannot live and grow on images and snippets of information alone. Sustained reading of texts is a vital component of the acquisition of knowledge and the health of the intellect. No amount of obfuscation can nullify this fact or the fact that lengthy texts are, and will continue to be, best read in the form of print on paper. Our choice is stark. We either nurture the minds of our children by teaching them to read and love reading or we condemn them to a life of, at best, functional literacy in an image-sedated underclass.

I will foster reading in children and be devoted
to increasing literacy in society.

147

Are Libraries Dangerous?

People can lose their lives in libraries.
They ought to be warned.

—Saul Bellow, quoted in
The Reader's Quotation Book

 The histories of great libraries are replete with tales of men and women for whom the library was the center of their existence. It is as though the library loomed larger for these people—eccentric, deluded, obsessional, fixated on a subject to the exclusion of all others—than for the common run of library user. Some used the library as a harbor from life's storms and nothing more; others did serious research and wrote good books; yet others made notes for year after year right up to the day when they walked out of the library never to return. Almost all these people were harmless and different from the average user only in their bibliophilia and the intensity of their interests. Such characters are common in great libraries but even the majority of us—who do not work in the likes of the Library of Congress or the Bibliothèque Nationale—have our own stories of those who haunt our library day in and day out. Is it the library that changes their lives or are their lives made easier because they have the library as a refuge?

I will cherish the variety of those
who love libraries.

Ten

The Wider World

The A.D.A.

Love is the fulfilling of the law.

—St. Paul's Epistle to the Romans

The Americans with Disabilities Act, passed in 1990, is the most comprehensive law of its kind in the world. The second of its five sections (Title II) is an elaboration of the right of all citizens to have equal access to all public services, in this case without any barrier, physical or otherwise, that would prevent persons with disabilities (widely defined) from enjoyment of those services. Title II applies, obviously, to all publicly funded libraries, which, in these days, means almost all libraries. The A.D.A. mandates a series of positive actions for each library—some of which involve considerable expenditure of time, money, and human resources (physical remodeling, purchase of special equipment, appointment of a compliance officer, and the adoption and promulgation of grievance procedures, among others). There are those who see these as more bureaucratic regulation, but they are, in truth, mechanisms necessary to allow our disabled users the same right of free access to knowledge and information that we are pledged to provide to all.

*I will gladly honor the letter and
the spirit of the A.D.A.*

The Choice

Look at the stars! Look, look up at the skies!
—Gerard Manley Hopkins, *The Starlight Night*

 I read yesterday that astronomers now estimate there are 400 billion stars in the universe for each human alive today. As many galaxies are now known as there are stars in our galaxy. Faced with such immensity, what are we to think and do? There are two paths. One is of a crushing sense of insignificance spawning fear, despair, and nihilism. The other is of the life of the mind and of the spirit. Each of us, religious or humanist, can tread that path and celebrate the knowledge, understanding, and wisdom that humans have achieved or discovered, recorded, and made available in libraries. Unrecorded knowledge benefits very few for a very short time. Knowledge recorded and preserved benefits the ages. That is why we librarians have only one choice in the face of the immense universe.

I will preserve knowledge for the ages.

Bookstores

The Bookshop has a thousand books
All colors, hues, and tinges
And every cover is a door
That turns on magic hinges.

—Nancy Byrd Turner, *The Bookshop*

 Bookstores come in all shapes and sizes. Their latest metamorphosis is the mega-bookstore (Barnes & Noble, Borders, Waterstones) but there are still musty secondhand bookstores run by scholars, rogues, eccentrics, and just plain book lovers. There are also airport bookstalls; the kind of bookstore "lite" that you find in shopping malls; bookstores specializing in mysteries, cookbooks, or military histories; and places that traffic in greeting cards and calendars alongside best-sellers. Despite the published fears of some, not a one of them is in competition with libraries. We must all have had the experience of going into a bookstore and meeting one or more library "regulars" who recognize us but cannot quite place us away from the library context. No, readers are readers and get their fixes wherever and whenever they can. A civilized community is one that has libraries and a range of bookstores. One of the shrinking number of delights of big city life is the almost endless supply of places for book lovers to frequent.

I will love bookstores for themselves and
because they complement our work.

Story Time

Thy loving smile will surely hail
The love gift of a fairy-tale.

—Lewis Carroll, introduction to
Through the Looking Glass

 The storyteller has been a figure of influence and respect in human communities since speech began. We think particularly of children loving stories, but the popularity of audiobooks is a modern manifestation of the deep-seated desire to hear stories that live in all of us—no matter our age. Time after time, surveys of public perceptions of public libraries have shown that children's services rank above all other priorities (followed by book collections and library buildings). Despite all our innovations in services and programs, it could well be that the oldest service that we give—reading or telling stories to children—is the best public relations we can get. Of course, it is not only PR; we read to children to educate, amuse, and widen horizons and to further literacy. We also read to children to satisfy an atavistic need—to watch their rapt faces and to re-create those circles of early humans around a cave fire listening to the shaman conjure wonders in words.

I will read to children for myself
as well as for them.

Multiple Identities

No, Groucho is not my real name.
I'm breaking it in for a friend.

—Attributed to Groucho Marx,
Penguin Dictionary of Modern Quotations

Legend has it that Queen Victoria was so entranced by the first of the *Alice* books that she asked its author, the Reverend Charles Lutwidge Dodgson, to be sure to send her his next book as soon as it was published. Months later, the Queen was not amused to receive a massive tome on symbolic logic. Although the Reverend Dodgson was indisputably only one person, he was two authors—Dodgson the scholar and Lewis Carroll, the fantasist of genius.

The Queen's disappointment was the result of a problem that has long been known to cataloguers but has only recently been addressed in cataloguing rules. There are really no new issues in cataloguing, just better solutions to old problems. Surely the recognition of multiple bibliographic identities inhabiting the same person is such a better solution. Such multiple identities may be of interest to the biographer and bibliographer. They are of no interest to the general reader who may well enjoy the novels of Gore Vidal and not care a whit for the mystery stories of Edgar Box or that they are one and the same person.

I will support rules that use the forms
of name my library's users know.

155

International Book Sharing

My country is the world and my religion is to do good.

—Thomas Paine, *The Rights of Man*

 Books know no boundaries. Many libraries participate in programs by which books they no longer need are donated to developing countries. There is a thirst for reading and a desire to acquire knowledge in those countries that puts most of us to shame. We live surrounded by books of all kinds on every topic under the sun—books that we can afford to buy or books that we can easily borrow from a local library. If we do not read it is because we choose not to. It is hard, in this and other areas of life, to imagine what it must be like to be deprived of what we take for granted; to be an intellectually lively student or general reader in a place in which a current book is a rare luxury. We should remember that, in many countries, the power supply is erratic at best and telecommunications rudimentary. Therefore, a good book is a far more reliable friend than even the most modern computer. Book sharing must be done with discrimination—even the book-poor have no use for the outdated or worthless discards—but there are many older books that fill real needs. Let us, by all means, send useful books to developing countries and share the recorded knowledge that we have in such abundance.

I will share our wealth of recorded knowledge with the rest of the world.

UnBooks?

*Even bad books are books and
therefore sacred.*

—Gunther Grass,
Rasputin and the Alphabet

 Recent *New York Times* best-seller lists have contained (among all the histories, biographies, social commentaries, political books, and other "legitimate" genres) books of cartoons, self-help books, collections of humorous columns, books "by" TV stars, diet books, and hagiographies of the wealthy. Very few of these had been or would be reviewed in the *Times*. People get pleasure from these books or they would not be published. Does that mean they should all be in libraries? Even public libraries need to tread carefully in this minefield, because some of these genres (e.g., diet books) are represented by enormous numbers of publications.

Academic libraries used to have an out—that of buying only materials that support the curricula. As curricula expand, that rationale crumbles. What of the criminology student who wants the books on the Simpson criminal trial? What of the nutrition program that demands diet books? Is it elitist to extend the idea of good books and bad books to good genres and bad genres? Do we thus encourage collection development policies that, without a qualm, admit the buying of mediocre histories and the rejection of good books of cartoons or useful self-help books? We study popular culture now and our collections should reflect and aid those studies.

*I will collect popular genres because
they illuminate our times.*

157

Time Machines

A book is . . . your own time machine that can transport you from the present to the past and into the future.

—Sol M. Malkin, quoted on the cover of
AB: Bookman's Weekly

 No lengthy text is ever read just in order to acquire information. A reader, in her or his lifelong quest to become more literate, reads to know and understand life better. In that involvement with texts, the truly interactive activity of reading can teach you about yourself, about society, about spirituality, about the past, and about what is to be. It is not just great novels that take a person to other realms, to new levels of understanding. Any worthwhile text, read attentively, will cause the reader to know more than before and in that knowledge is power—the power of self-improvement and understanding. We can read a biography and know ourselves better; a history text to know what the future will be like; and a book on genetics to know more about what it means to be human.

I will encourage reading of substantive texts as a path to knowledge.

Reports, Statistics, and All That Jazz

*He uses statistics as a drunken man uses
a lamp-post—for support rather than
illumination.*

—Andrew Lang, quoted in
Alan L. MacKay's
The Harvest of a Quiet Eye

 There is nothing at all wrong with making library
administration more efficient and organized. There is
a price to be paid, though, for the organized approach.
We must endure the hideous jargon of modern management;
attend more meetings than should reasonably be asked of
anyone; and produce more reports, statistics, and plans than
we ever dreamed of when in library school. Perhaps the latter
are a necessary evil. Necessary or not, how can we escape the
choice between doing something or writing about doing
something? Modern automated systems produce more statistics than we can use, but at least they do not have to be com-
piled laboriously as in the past. However, machines cannot
produce the mission statements, goals, strategies to achieve
goals, plans, and reports on plans that make up the endless
annual cycle of paper piled upon paper. The result is people
with new phobias—report anxiety, planner's angst, fear of statistics—all the symptoms of those compelled to write more
than anyone can or wishes to read.

*I will distinguish between useful and useless
reports, plans, and statistics.*

159

Technology as Religion

Technology is sublime and horrific, divine and satanic, inevitable and unpredictable. It is no wonder that it seems as if technology were this era's religion . . .

—Edward Rothstein, "The Future Works, Sometimes," *New York Times,* 1997

 The idea of life as it was 75, 100, 200 years ago has a number of attractions, but few of us would wish to be transported back to those times for at least one simple reason: technology (particularly medical technology) has made life in developed countries today more physically pleasant than it has ever been.

We have paid and continue to pay a price for that comfort. The ease of movement afforded by the automobile is paid for daily in pollution. The technological advances that have given us global mass communication have also given us a stultified culture and children poisoned mentally by visual schlock and physically by the fast food that they are taught to crave. The list of dualities is endless and rendered ever more perplexing by "technology as religion." Its adherents preach perfectibility, inevitability, and redemption—an escape from the sorrows of today; pie in the sky *before* we die. Librarians should be agnostics outside this church—seeing technology as a tool to be used, not a brazen god to be worshiped.

I will not be mastered by technology but use it to achieve good ends.

"Thin Places"

Dark brow'd sophist, come not anear;
All the place is holy ground.

—Alfred Tennyson, *The Poet's Mind*

 Joseph Campbell wrote about "thin places"—places on earth at which the curtain between the normal and the paranormal can be lifted. These are places that, because of their history and associations, have a sacred quality that causes the visitor to meditate on the perception that there is more to human existence than daily joys and sorrows. Campbell was, of course, thinking of, among others, Glastonbury (believed by many to be the Avalon of King Arthur), the Black Hills of South Dakota, the rock dwellings of the southwestern United States, temple sites of East Asia, Ankor Wat in Cambodia, and of great historic churches and other buildings. I would suggest that many libraries have something of this quality. I do not mean only old, famous libraries in which great people have read and written great books but also humbler libraries used by generations of people unknown to history. There is something of the sacred in the least library: something that speaks to us of the human soul as well as the human mind, of the continuity of memory and achievement, of the joy of youth and the wisdom of age.

I will not relinquish the sanctity, the magic,
that libraries share with other "thin places."

84, Charing Cross Road

*The aim is to live lucidly in a world in which
dispersion is the rule.*

—Albert Camus, *Les Cahiers (The Notebooks)*

 I could not love anyone who did not love Helene
Hanff's *84, Charing Cross Road.* Ms. Hanff died at the
age of eighty after a lifetime dedicated to collecting
and reading books. She was a great autodidact, reveling in
both the sensuous and intellectual pleasures of the books that
were the center of her life. It is, by now, a familiar story—this
woman with a passion for reading who wanted to acquire and
cherish the very best editions of the texts she loved. She
entered into a long-distance relationship with a London book-
seller who supplied her with books and, in the course of of a
long correspondence, with the kind of friendship that is nur-
tured by shared enthusiasm.

Helene Hanff was a writer made famous by her love
of books—a love made palpable by her writer's skill. She died
in the studio apartment filled with her books in which she
lived alone for most of her long life—a life that contained the
happiness that only comes from a passion fulfilled.

*I will honor the enthusiasms and passions
that make life worth living.*

Eleven

Practicalities

I will enjoy the sight of well-bound books

Bindings

 For half a millennium, a book has been defined as printed pages collated and bound together. Much attention has been paid to the paper on which we print because of the tragedy of the acidic paper that was used in mass publishing for more than 100 years and created a preservation crisis. The print itself is the subject of thousands of books and manuals—from hand printing through metal type to computer-generated print and desktop publishing. Less attention is paid to binding—even the paper binding that makes the technological and economic miracle of the paperback possible. This is despite the fact that binding, similar in most ways to the fine binding of today, is known to have existed in the first century of the Common Era—earlier than either print or paper. Hand binding is still practiced but has declined in the face of mechanization. Publishers know that bindings are not as important to sales as flashy covers but the good ones ensure their books are bound with quality. We are all familiar with, but few give much thought to, the library bindings whose solid colors decorate many miles of our shelves. Nevertheless, they tell us that these books are for use.

I will enjoy the sight of well-bound books.

Dress for Success?

Those who make their dress a principal part of themselves will, in general, become of no more value than their dress.

—William Hazlitt, *On the Clerical Character*

 Long ago, the first library in which I worked had a strict dress code for its staff, strictly enforced. Women were forbidden to wear colored hose, trousers, sandals, or anything much more outlandish than blouses, skirts, and sensible shoes. Men had to wear light-colored shirts, ties, dark trousers, and sports jackets or a suit. (For all I recall, short hair was prescribed—but it was universal anyway in those pre-Beatles days.) Oddly enough, the women alone had to wear blue lab coats in a peculiarly nasty shiny artificial fabric. Perhaps their clothes were thought to be more expensive and in need of protection. Even to me, this seems like news from a century ago, such has been the change in customs and attitudes. Now, the merest hint that, say, an Oakland Raiders t-shirt is inappropriate for a reference desk would be treated as an infringement on life, liberty, and the pursuit of happiness. The fine line between informality and scruffiness has never been finer, but better a cheerful scruffiness than a dour correctness. Studies show that some people are still intimidated by libraries and librarians and, if for no other reason, the new casualness is good if it helps to reduce barriers to library use.

I will dress for work in a manner that is comfortable for me and for the library's users.

No Food, No Drink

A Book of Verses underneath the Bough,
A Jug of Wine, a Loaf of Bread . . .

—Edward Fitzgerald,
The Rubaiyat of Omar Khayyam

 The stereotypical librarian is a puritan about food and drink. The minatory signs that pepper our libraries are regarded by many users as the outward signs of the control-freak within. The sad fact is, of course, that food and drink are poor companions for the books themselves, but excellent companions for the reader. They are also much loved by pests and vermin. Library users who cannot see why they may not eat and drink in the library but are welcome to pay to do so in the local mega-bookstore are missing two points. The mega-store is selling the food and drink to lure you to buy their wares. Also, they undoubtedly write off damage to their stock as part of the cost of doing business. Those excellent institutions are not, as we are, in the preservation business but in the business business. What is the poor librarian to do? Seek, probably in vain, to ban all food and drink? Open a library cafe? Restrict eating and drinking to a special area? Just one set of conundrums among many for us in this age of rethinking.

I will balance the real conservation needs
of the collection and the comfort and ease
of my library's users.

167

Coral Reefs

*Small sands the mountain, moments make
    the year,
And trifles life.*

—Edward Young, *Satire*

 Just as a life is an accumulation of events, details, trifles, a library collection is the cumulative result of a huge number of individual decisions. Collections are built by people and, truth to tell, by happenstance. Collection development policies will guide decisions made over many years but, in fact, most are records of what has happened and projections based on precedent rather than plan. Just as multitudes of coral build mighty reefs—classic examples of the whole being greater than the sum of its parts—library collections take on lives of their own and achieve uniqueness as an unintended consequence. The contributions and interests of librarians and library users long retired and long forgotten live on as parts of a structure that is different from all others and, in retrospect, possesses an integrity and wholeness that could never have resulted from a rigid plan.

*I will remember that every library
collection is unique.*

Circulation

Come and take choice of all my library
And so beguile thy sorrow.

—William Shakespeare, *Titus Andronicus*

 Between the handwritten ledgers of long ago and the automated circulation modules of today lie an amazing variety of systems used to record lending and borrowing, overdues and fines, "holds" and loan periods, and the rest of the data we use to safeguard library collections. I cannot imagine anyone ever writing a history of circulation systems, but it would be a fascinating excursion into library history, technology, and attitudes toward users and collections.

We often take circulation systems for granted but they and the people who operate them are important for a number of reasons. The genius of the online catalogue lies in linking catalogue records and circulation records and, thereby, answering the most important user question—"can I have this item now?" Many of the users of larger libraries have no contact with anyone in the library other than circulation staff, and how those staff treat those users is a major factor in the public perception of the library. Circulation staff are the front line of preservation. It is they who make the crucial decision to put material back on the shelves or send it to be repaired or bound.

I will understand and support the value
of circulation staff and systems.

Filing

Filing is concerned with the past . . .

—Katherine Whitehorn,
Sunday Best

 Few of us file in catalogues today, but retrieval systems and displays still have all the old familiar problems of "Mc" and "Mac"; numbers and letters; letters with accents; letters that do not appear in our Roman alphabet or in any Roman alphabet; titles beginning with articles; and on and on. The drudgery may be gone, but filing problems are always with us.

The greatest triumph of process over practicality I ever saw concerned filing. The scene was a great research library with a multimillion-card catalogue. (Their two organized filing backlogs would have made respectable catalogues for lesser libraries, but that is another story.) Many people toiled over the maintenance of this bibliographic behemoth and they obeyed a strict hierarchy. Cards were filed "over the rod" to be checked by supervisors who would, if all were well, pull the rod out and let the cards nestle in their allotted places. If the card was misfiled, it was moved to the correct place and the offense noted. In especially intractable cases, a woman with thirty years experience—a kind of Filing Czarina—would descend from her office and make the final decision.

The thing that was overlooked was, of course, that if you needed thirty years experience to file a card, you would need thirty years experience to be able to *find* that card.

I will prize practicality over process.

Indexes and Indexing

He writes indexes to perfection.

—Oliver Goldsmith, *Citizen of the World*

 Some books live or die by their indexes. An index can be the determining factor in whether a reference book is useful. I have a cookbook that contains great recipes but has an index so eccentric that it is easier to memorize the recipes than to hunt for them. On the other hand, I have just read a long biography packed with detail and possessing a marvelous index that enables the reader to locate any fact or incident with ease. The Anglo-American tradition of serious writing and publishing calls for an extensive "scholarly apparatus" (indexes, footnotes, citations, and bibliographies) and it is always a shock to read continental European, especially French, books that lack footnotes or indexes. There have been a number of attempts to automate indexing, and there is no doubt that indexes have improved greatly over the last fifty years. However, indexing cannot be mechanized and its largely anonymous practitioners need much flair and intuition to accompany the automated approach. Pity the poor indexer! Most readers take good indexes for granted and curse bad ones and, in either event, give little thought to the people who created them.

I will appreciate the work of the Unknown Indexer.

Interlibrary Loan

All for one, one for all.

> —Alexandre Dumas,
> *The Three Musketeers*

 The greatest achievement of library automation is the OCLC online union catalogue. In libraries, as in the rest of life, you never know where a path will take you. The idea of some Ohio college libraries getting together to share cataloguing data grew into a vast international database for disseminating catalogue records to libraries everywhere. In the course of becoming this world resource, OCLC created the first truly effective global union catalogue, which, in turn, is an essential part of the national and international resource-sharing infrastructure.

OCLC's print predecessor, the 685-volume *National Union Catalog,* is a monument to bibliography and cooperation but, on the day it was published, contained no title that was less than *twenty-five* years old. Compare this to the OCLC union catalogue, as up-to-date as yesterday's cataloguing. With the OCLC database at its core, today's structure of local, state, regional, national, and international resource sharing is a Web that dwarfs any present achievement of the electronic Web, for all the latter's glitter and glamour.

> *I will participate and support gladly*
> *all cooperation—local and global.*

"Indecency" Online

No morality can be founded on authority . . .

—A. J. Ayer, *Essay on Humanism*

 As each new form of communication becomes common, the dreary cycle of censorship is reborn and must run its course. Today, there is a hysteria abroad in the land about indecency on the Internet. It has swept up libraries and librarians because we provide access to the Net for those who have no access otherwise—including the poor, those who lack computer skills, and children. The first national product of this wave of censorship was the Communications Decency Act of 1996, soon challenged as unconstitutional—as it patently is. Since its passing, legislators in no fewer than seventeen states have rushed in and proposed various ways of controlling what the citizens can see and read on the Net. Much of this huffing and puffing comes under the guise of protecting minors and is the fatal confluence of two mastering desires of lawmakers—to be up-to-date and to protect their view of public morality. We can take the long view and predict safely that this particular periodic fit of public moralizing will soon peter out as legislators find something even newer to fuss about. In the short term, though, it is right that library groups, from ALA on down, and individual librarians take up the cudgels once again in defense of the right to know and, oh yes, the Constitution of the United States.

> *I will resist attempts to restrict the availability of knowledge and information on the Net.*

Fifty Cent Technology

Imagine if everybody had a computer for
$9,000 and you were stuck by a table every
time you had to learn anything or read any-
thing . . . And all of a sudden somebody
invented a whole new thing— a newspaper!
You know what would happen? Everybody
would say "What an invention! A newspaper!
For half a dollar you got the same thing!"
Not only that, you can take it wherever you
want to go.

—Jackie Mason in his
one-man show "Love Thy Neighbor"

 Which is more foolish—abandoning old things just because they are old or rejecting new things just because they are new? To point out the truth that computers are not always the answer is not to reject comput-ers completely. To say that newspapers have a valuable role in society and in individual communities *and* that the technology upon which they are based—print on paper—is the best and most cost-effective means of fulfilling that role is not to be re-actionary. Compare the ease with which one can scan a news-paper for items that are of interest with the slowness and impracticality of scanning their electronic versions. You will soon come to the conclusion that computers cannot compete as far as the general reader is concerned.

I will look at the practicalities
of communication objectively.

Descriptive Cataloguing in 131 Words

Simplify, simplify.

—Henry David Thoreau,
Where I Have Lived and What I Lived For

 I was one of those fortunate few library students who took to cataloguing from the beginning. (Good teachers helped.) I know that, for many, cataloguing is a course to be avoided and its sacred texts objects to be feared. The secret is that the secrets of descriptive cataloguing can be summarized in a few sentences.

> A catalogue entry has three parts: an access point (heading) that gets you to the record you want; a description that tells you whether this is the material you want; a location to tell you where the item is and whether it is available. The formulation of access points is based on two ideas: that there is a work (a human creation) of which the object described (book, video, electronic document, etc.) is a manifestation; and the names of the creators of that work should be the access points. The description is formulated according to simple rules that are standard for all media. The location tells you how the library stores its materials and makes them available. The catalogue is the sum of all the entries made in accordance with these ideas.

That is all there is to it, and AACR2, MARC, and the rest are just elaborations on the themes.

I will gain insight into my work by understanding the essentials of what we do.

Central Libraries vs. Branch Libraries

. . . and sing among the branches.

—Psalms 104:3

 Public library systems all over have been faced with a cruel dilemma in these hard times. Their budgets tell them that they are unable to support both a full-service central library and their network of branch libraries. What to do? Prune the hours and services of the central library and keep all the branches open? Put such resources as there are into the central library and scale back or close the branches?

Each approach has its advantages. Keeping one library (the central library) open and fully functioning ensures that the town or county has at least one locus of full library service. Keeping the branches going preserves services of great importance to specific communities. As usual, different interests are affected differently. The branches matter to the elderly, to children, to homemakers, to the poor—to anyone who finds it difficult or impossible to drive downtown or to another town. A good full-service central library is a boon to the mobile and the affluent, to businesses, students, and researchers.

Would that all public library systems could afford a flourishing central library and flourishing branches. Most cannot, however, and those who have to make such hard choices deserve our sympathy and support.

I will try to balance all the interests
of all the people who use my library.

Twelve

Eternal Promises

Sunrise

*Early one morning, just as the sun
was rising . . .*

—English folk song

 Some few winter and early spring days, when the air is clear and the time is right, I see the sun rise over the Sierra Nevada on my way to work. The mountains are so high that the sky is light minutes before long rays of sunshine appear. Then the edge of the sun peers over the jagged peaks and rises quickly until it hangs—a huge crimson ball—above the mountains and over the valley farmlands and houses. When I see this sight, I always think of the metaphor of constancy it embodies—the eternal promise of rebirth. The sun rises over the Sierra each day whether the people west of the mountains see it or not. When we do see it, the rhythms of permanence are made manifest. There is something that appeals to the soul, as well as the eye, about such natural sights—to the something in us that hungers for continuity. From that feeling comes the need and desire for permanence and unchanging values from libraries. When we open the library each morning, it is not just a useful action. We are in harmony with the cycles of life and the unconscious expectations of humanity—just by being there, as always.

*I will dedicate my library work
to a constancy of values and spirit.*

Library Time

*Never before have we had so little time
to do so much.*

—Franklin Delano Roosevelt, radio address

 Different libraries exist in different times and have different seasons. We do not inhabit a 9 to 5, five-day workweek world. Much of our work time is the leisure time of most people and the unusual work time of others. Even different libraries of the same type have different rhythms of time. A public library in a city business district may be hectic during the weekdays, used heavily by the daytime population, while its suburban branch is busy in the evenings and weekends when the central city is empty of workers. Children's libraries have their high days of story hours and puppet shows and their slack times when only the most determined young readers come. Academic libraries, governed by the peculiarities of the academic calendar, come to life at the end of the long summer and in late winter after the New Year. They also shape their lives according to the social lives and study habits of students—those odd creatures who shun the library on Friday evenings and Saturdays but swarm the library on Sunday evenings impelled by the panic induced by an idle weekend. We all construct our own chronologies around the needs of our users and measure our days differently from the workaday world.

*I will provide service at times when
users need it.*

Reminders of Continuity

> *Libraries are reservoirs of strength, grace, and*
> *wit, reminders of continuity, lakes of mental*
> *energy, neither warm nor cold, light nor dark.*
> *The pleasure they give is steady, unorgastic,*
> *reliable, deep, and long-lasting. In any library*
> *in the world, I am at home—unselfconscious,*
> *still, and absorbed.*

> —Germaine Greer, "Still in Melbourne
> January 1987," in her *Daddy, We Hardly Knew You*

 A library is much more than the sum of its collections and services to a library lover. Ms. Greer writes of the essential qualities—continuity, reliability, accessibility—that make such people at home the moment they step into any library anywhere. In fifty years, I have visited libraries large and small in many countries of Europe and in the United States, Canada, Australia, Japan, and Korea. I know well the continuity that stretches between the first library that I remember well—Golders Green branch library in 1947—and all the diverse libraries that I have used and in which I have worked in the years since. There are physical similarities and a sameness of atmosphere, but beyond those in every library there is a sense of possibility, a potential for wonder. For all our orderliness and organization, for all the stillness and quiet, just below the surface there is the anarchic impulse that keeps us believing that at any moment our lives may be changed.

> *I will retain the wonder and sense of possibility*
> *that libraries hold for their users.*

Where Love Begins

> *. . . A library is also a place where love begins.*
>
> —Rudolfo Anaya,
> "In Commemoration,"
> in *The Magic of Words*

The quotation is from Rudolfo Anaya's wonderful essay commemorating the University of New Mexico's one-millionth volume. He was referring to writing love notes in his high school library for fellow students at a dime apiece but there are many kinds of love and all of them can begin in a library—a real library such as that of UNM as recollected by Anaya. "There I found peace. The carved vigas decorating the ceiling, the solid wooden tables and chairs, and the warm adobe color of the stucco . . . With books scattered around me, I could read and doze and dream." How long would love and dreams—the dreams that inspire art—survive in the sterility of the virtual library?

I will prize the love evoked by libraries.

Occam's Management Theory

*Entities should not be multiplied
without necessity.*

—Attributed to William of Occam

 As have almost all librarians, I have lived through many management fads imported from the business world to live uneasily in our public service environment until they wither away and are replaced by the next trendy acronym. From MBO to TQM, they are all a combination of common sense, jargon, and suspect theorizing. Once one is beyond the verbiage and theories, the commonsense element of each is remarkably similar to the others. Participation, tolerance of other views, flexibility, service orientation, abolition of hierarchies—they all add up to what a friend calls "applied feminism." To my mind, none of them is as downright useful as the fourteenth century rationalist wisdom of William of Occam. What better way to look at library organization than to question the necessity of each and every unit? What better guide could there be to writing a job description? Now if only old William ("the Invincible Doctor") had a snappy acronym and a marketing plan.

I will cast a cold eye on management fads.

What Is "Information"?

All information is imperfect.

—Jacob Bronowski, *The Ascent of Man*

Politicians speak at length of the "Information Age." Library schools are library schools no more but "schools of library and information studies" (in the case of those who are not entirely with the trend and still carry the word "library" in their names). Universities are being asked, by librarians among others, to teach and promote "information literacy." There is something called "information science," though I have seen no evidence to prove it anything other than "librarianship practiced by men" (in librarian Ellen Crosby's marvelous phrase). Librarians are advised to become "information professionals." We are told "information is power" and that we are moving from a society that makes things to one based on information services.

Missing from all this is a satisfactory definition of "information"—this omnipotent, omnipresent force. Dictionaries are no help—all I have consulted use "knowledge" and "information" interchangeably in their definitions. It sometimes appears that information is so powerful as to be unknowable and must simply be accepted with the fervor of true faith. I will attempt to be rational and propose that there are only two possible definitions. The first states that information comprehends all human communication in all forms. This, of course, solves nothing. If a painting by Rembrandt is visual information and a novel by Dickens textual information, what

does a term like "Information Age" mean and what does an "information scientist" study? The second definition comports with normal understanding. It states that information consists of data (facts) and small, discrete factual descriptions. If, as I believe, it is a satisfactory definition, it punctures the "information revolution" balloon.

I will think my way past bogus "revolutions."

Universal Bibliographic Control

*Government and cooperation are in all things
the law of life.*

—John Ruskin, *Unto This Last*

 Universal Bibliographic Control (UBC), launched by
IFLA in 1974, is by common consent the most ambi-
tious international program in the history of librarianship. It was subsequently adopted by UNESCO and is the offi-
cial policy of national libraries and library organizations
throughout the world. The aims of UBC can be stated quite
simply. They are to ensure universal access to current, standardized bibliographic data for all publications from all countries. This comprehensive goal requires an infrastructure that
enables cooperation within and between countries and universal agreement on standards. All cataloguers will, and all librarians should, sympathize with an idea at the heart of UBC—that
each item should be catalogued once and once only in its country of origin and the resulting record be made available speedily to all the world's libraries. This is where standards come in.
The international standards MARC and ISBD ensure a substantial agreement on much of the UBC record. AACR2, used
in many countries and influential in many more, assures a measure of agreement on names and titles as access points. Subject
access, alas, lacks such standardization.

It is easy to be daunted by the intricate details of international standards and cooperation, but we should not lose

sight of the essential rightness of UBC. It is the future of international librarianship—its achievements are to be celebrated and its promise encouraged.

> *I will support cooperation and standardization at all levels because, though difficult, it moves us toward universal access.*

Illuminated Manuscripts

What in me is dark
Illumine; what is low, raise and support.

—John Milton, *Paradise Lost*

 Beginning in the depths of the Dark Ages (in the fourth and fifth centuries of the Common Era), European monks produced what are undoubtedly the most beautiful multimedia works ever—illuminated manuscripts. They continued to do so for more than 1,000 years; an example of sustained creativity of a high order that may never be equaled. No one who has ever seen an illuminated manuscript will soon forget the subtle interweaving of text and illustration, the abundance of life, and the almost preternatural vividness of the colors. One is in the presence of great art, of sophisticated high culture. The texts are religious yet the iconography includes phenomena of everyday medieval life (clothing, fruits, flowers, animals, furniture) as well as beasts and devils that seem to have more to do with paganism than Christianity. You find this splendid mixture in even the most overtly religious manuscripts—the prayer books known as Books of Hours.

The craftsmanship of those anonymous monks and the care with which they chose their materials can be seen in how the manuscripts still glow with light and life across the centuries. Though the work of illuminating and scribing was slow and almost unimaginably painstaking, illuminated man-

uscripts were produced in large numbers and many hundreds still exist. Their existence is a tribute to the durability of the materials used and the inks and paints chosen. It should also be a source of pride in our profession, that librarians were foremost in gathering, protecting, and preserving these treasures.

> *I will honor the heritage of those who preserved civilization's legacy.*

The Librarianship of Love

Love is, above all, the gift of oneself.

—Jean Anouilh, *Ardéle*

 We can and do spend too much time worrying whether librarianship is a craft or an art, a job or a profession. Irrespective of whether it is one or the other, all or none, librarianship has three major values: service, intellectual freedom, and preservation of the cultural record. We seek to serve each user of the library by supplying the collections that she or he needs and the assistance necessary to gain the most from those collections. We stand with every legal expression of thought and the unalienable right to make those expressions. We care deeply about the preservation and onward transmission of the cultural record and do what we can to ensure that the baton is not dropped on our lap.

These are noble ideals and they do not arise from a void. Many librarians hew to these values because they are altruistic; others because they think of them as a natural part of the profession they chose. My belief is that the force behind these ideas and the reason why so many struggle to overcome adversities and realize these values is, dare I say it?—love. A committed librarian is a person who loves humanity and seeks to help individuals and society; a person who loves learning and the achievements of humankind; and, above all, a person who loves truth. There *is* a librarianship of love and, often unknowingly, we practice it daily.

I will hold in my heart the values that define librarianship.

Manuscripts

Ye shall see how large a letter I have written
unto you with mine own hand.

—St. Paul's Epistle to the Galatians, 6:11

 I am writing this with a Japanese fine point pen on a pad of white paper with blue lines at my ancient, cluttered wooden desk. When done, I will type these words into a word processor, editing as I go. Increasingly, writers skip the first step and compose using only the computer. The telephone, e-mail, and word processing are common tools and few people write holograph letters let alone lengthy manuscripts. When handwritten pages have entirely vanished from the earth, the world of scholarship will be impoverished and a specialized branch of librarianship will cease to exist.

Who would wish to be a historian or literary scholar in 2097? The trail would be stone cold and the most one could hope for would be photographs, videos, and audiotapes. I once had the pleasure of reviewing the manuscripts of a justly acclaimed poet. There were drafts written on the backs of envelopes, letters from colleagues with annotations in the poet's hand, versions of translations with commentary from collaborators, blue carbon copies on onion paper—all the ephemera of a creative life and the very stuff of scholarly enquiry. When we have abandoned handwriting in favor of the evanescence of speech and electronic mail, there will be no such traces of important lives.

I will encourage the collection of
holographic materials.

191

Singular Strengths

*A library is the delivery room for the birth of
ideas, a place where history comes to life.*

—Norman Cousins, quoted in the *ALA Bulletin*

 It is often asserted that no two snowflakes are alike,
though I cannot imagine how you would prove it. It
is also true that no two libraries are alike—collections,
staff, buildings, programs, services differ in ways large and
small. Most of these differences are of little consequence, but
each library has at least one particular strength—something
that sets it apart and makes it uniquely valuable. That strength
can be in staff or a program, but these are things that change
over time. Enduring strengths are usually found in collections.
There have been many collection overlap studies over many
years, and without exception the overlap between the collections of superficially similar libraries is much less than a casual
guess might suggest. This is a major strength of library resource sharing. Naturally, great libraries have more unique and
rare materials, but even the smallest library contains something special. These singular strengths are a response to each
library's community of users and, we should admit, the vaga-
ries of chance. However they come about, all libraries should
rejoice in, and build on, the elements that make them special.

*I will prize the unique aspects of my
library's collections.*

Closing Libraries

Architecture in general is frozen music.

—Friedrich von Schelling, *Philosophy of Art*

 It is sad to see a library building close and sadder still if the library is not going to be replaced. The first library in which I ever worked is no more. This impressive late Victorian building, for all its vaulting reference room and general reading area, also contained poky little offices, dark corridors, and tenebrous stacks that defied even modern lighting. When it closed, the staff and collections were moved to a then modern building which, not much more than thirty years later, is showing serious signs of wear.

In the late nineteenth and early twentieth centuries, civic and educational buildings were built to impress and to last. When we see them closed, converted, or demolished, there is an unsettling feeling of a crack in the fabric of community and of the shifting parameters of life that is the specialty of our times. Our utilitarian part says that outdated buildings should be replaced and that new buildings adapted to modern needs are infinitely preferable. I would venture that most librarians have another side to them—a side that mourns the passing of old library buildings and feels that the community's soul is less because of the closure of imposing stone structures and, if we are lucky, their replacement by library palaces of steel and glass.

I will strive to reconcile the utilitarian,
aesthetic, and spiritual aspects
of library work.

Epilogue

And so we meditate . . .

What will be the future of libraries and of learning? Where is the long road of civilization going to take us? Many of us dream that, in the future, learning and literacy will thrive as the acquisition of knowledge through reading is enhanced by technology married to print and other linear resources. In other words, the future will be a marriage of the best of the past and present, of books and bytes, of reading and technology.

There is another, curiously discontinuous, vision. The same people who call for literacy and lament that "Johnny can't read" (try cuts in public and school libraries as part of that problem!) also preach the "death of the book" and say that all that matters is information. According to them, we are moving into a postliterate society dominated by the image. In their future, the global village turns out to be populated by illiterates who have rejected learning and are lulled by 1,000-channel TV and other anti-intellectual sensory gratifications. Such populations are malleable and readily manipulated politically, financially, and socially.

Would it not be the ultimate irony if the postliterate society were to come to pass and the records of humankind came full circle? The journey from the few people of the Aurignacian-Perigordian Epoch in 18000 B.C. who left the graphic images of their lives on the walls of the Lascaux Cave to billions of modern humans solitary and sedated by flickering transitory images will have taken a long time but could scarcely be accounted an advance.

What is it to be? Enhanced and flourishing libraries combining the best of all kinds of recorded knowledge and information on the one hand or a global Lascaux Cave on the other? A new golden age of literacy and learning or the end of the text? For myself, I would prefer to live in a reality informed by dreams and possibilities than to cyber-surf into oblivion as a member of the largest and loneliest crowd in all human history.

Michael Gorman, dean of libraries at California State University at Fresno, has worked in libraries for some four decades on two continents. He is co-author with Walt Crawford of the best-selling *Future Libraries: Dreams, Madness, and Reality* (1995). A shaper of the Anglo-American Cataloguing Rules, he has won numerous awards and honors, including the Melvil Dewey Medal.